Life Without Ceilings

A Woman's Career in Computers

Mary L. Gorden

GREEN HAT PRESS

Green Hat Press

http://marylgorden.com

Copyright © 2016 Mary L Gorden
Photos copyright © 2016 Mary L Gorden
All Rights Reserved

This is a memoir.
It reflects the author's present recollections of the events of her life.
Some names have been invented. Some events have been combined
and some dialogue has been recreated.

~ Print & eBook Publication Management ~
Eva Long / Long On Books : eva@longonbooks.com
Interior Design / Jeffrey Duckworth: duckofalltrades.com
Cover Design / Kellee Ratzlaff: growthcollab.com

Print ISBN: 978-0-9977664-0-0
eISBN: 978-0-9977664-1-7
Library of Congress Control Number: 2016910846

Publisher's Cataloging-In-Publication Data
(Prepared by The Donohue Group, Inc.)

Names: Gorden, Mary L., 1944-
Title: Life without ceilings : a woman's career in computers / Mary L. Gorden.
Description: [Greenwood, California] : Green Hat Press, [2016]
Identifiers: LCCN 2016910846 | ISBN 978-0-9977664-0-0 (print) |
ISBN 978-0-9977664-1-7 (ebook)
Subjects: LCSH: Gorden, Mary L., 1944- | Women computer programmers--
Biography. | Women in technology--Biography. | LCGFT: Autobiographies.
Classification: LCC QA76.2.G67 A3 2016 (print) | LCC QA76.2.G67 (ebook)
DDC 005.1092--dc23

Printed in the U.S.A

*This story is dedicated to my brother John
who left us way too early.*

Contents

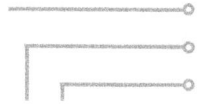

Dreams

ONCE IN A while a crazy dream becomes real. When I was in my early fifties—old enough to know the difference between dreams and reality—I longed to buy enough land to keep my horse in my own barn instead of at a boarding stable. My list of reasons why this was impossible was long. One big reason was that I had a high-powered job working as a systems designer in the international computer industry. The job required long hours and much travel. I was never sure what country I would be in at any given time. Plus I was deeply in debt from a divorce and didn't have money to spend on much of anything.

This lifestyle didn't fit well with being the primary custodian of a large, needy animal yet there was no question that being on the back of a running horse was the perfect antidote for the stresses of my job.

But times change. Obstacles disappear. In late 2000, I bought country property in California's Sierra Nevada foothills. Six months later, days before my fifty-seventh birthday, I retired from a career as one of the few women hired in the early years of the business computer industry. I sold my house in the San Francisco suburbs and moved over one hundred miles away from the people and places that had been part of my life for thirty-two years.

I gave the decision to move little thought. The right circumstances came along and I took advantage of them. It never occurred to me that there was anything strange or scary about this action until one of my friends expressed surprise at my courage in making the move.

But my life has taught me how to pick up and move. I grew up as a child in a navy family, and moving was the norm. I'd lived in more than a dozen different places before I was six years old and had moved to another seven areas of the country before I graduated from college. Why would another move scare me? A move to a different area of the country always brought me new experiences.

The many pleasures of country life in retirement with my horses also brought me women friends approximately my own age. I had not had a circle of friends like this since college. While I was working, the need to do high quality work quickly made the age and gender of my friends and colleagues irrelevant. Other criteria mattered more.

As I came to know these smart, capable women, my post-retirement friends, I was astonished at the limited number of fields in which they had worked. Most of them had been teachers and nurses. Some of them had been very successful. Two of the teachers had been principals, and one of those had supervised principals in a large school district. Though one of my friends had been an occupational therapist and had her own business, this was a far cry from the veterinarian she had wanted to be. Initially I thought one of my friends had been a lawyer as she expanded my knowledge of immigration law. But her knowledge of the law came from being the executive director of a non-profit law firm. She had started her career as a family counselor.

It seemed like I had followed a career path different from that of any of my friends. Still, when I was growing up, these women would have been held up to me as wonderful examples of what a woman could accomplish if she wanted to have a career. Those were the choices open to women when I was a girl.

When I was young I'd had another crazy dream. I wanted to do things with my life that interested me. I wanted to have an interesting life. The problem was that everything that interested me was something that "girls don't do." I didn't want to be a nurse; I wanted to be a doctor. I wanted to fix cars; I didn't want to be driven around in them. I didn't want to be a stewardess; I wanted to be a pilot. I heard the phrase "girls don't" a lot during my childhood when I answered the inevitable question from adults: What do you want to be when you grow up?

My plans for my future were restricted by having been born a girl in 1944. I was the oldest child in a large, close-knit navy family, and we were good Catholics. My father was a United States Naval Academy graduate, and my mother was a smart, educated woman who embraced her role as a good navy wife. It was an environment bound by tradition. There were clear boundaries on what a child was permitted to do. And there was a clear understanding of what you were to do as an adult. While these restrictions frustrated me, I wasn't a rebel. My life became a balancing act between quietly doing what I wanted to do and always agreeing I'd do the "right" thing when I grew up. My sister-in-law, Karen, put it best when she asked me many years later, "How did you escape?" My answer to her remains my answer today, "sheer dumb luck."

I do believe that some of your luck is of your own making. Being prepared for the eventuality that you want and taking advantage of a favorable opportunity is certainly a big part of what we call luck.

On the other hand, there is luck over which you have no control. I was fortunate enough to be born into a life where a family member helped to nourish a dream until it had roots to survive on its own. And more than once, someone stepped in at the right moment to help me do option B rather than option A. And over the long run, option B turned out to be so much better than anyone could have imagined at the time.

And another piece of good fortune: I was born in the 1940s, not ten years earlier, when all of the story I'm about to share with you would have been impossible.

Girls Don't

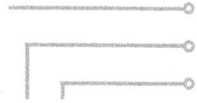

Chicago

I HEARD MOM calling me to come in. But I was in no
hurry. My younger brother, John, and I were playing
with our toy cars in one of the piles of sand around our
still incomplete apartment complex. By 1950, the massive
building boom that followed World War II had not finished
building all the houses that would be needed for the families of the children who would become known as the "baby
boomers." But for two children, six and four, the unfinished
building site was a wonderful play area. We built roads in
the sand and drove our cars and trucks on those roads. No
straight roads for us, lots of ups and downs and plenty of
curves. "Mary," Mom called again, "It's time to go back to
your grandparents." Just then my knee collided with a large
piece of broken glass. There was blood everywhere.

"Oh, wow," John said, "Your knee is a mess, does it
hurt?" Even as a little boy, he was concerned about others.

"No, I'm fine." I was more upset about the end of our automotive adventure than about my knee. John followed me as I hobbled up to the apartment building, my leg and sock getting stained crimson.

"You came quickly today," Mom said before she noticed my leg. "Do we need to take her to the doctor?" she asked Mackie, my grandfather, who had arrived to take me back to his apartment.

"No need," he replied, "we'll just bandage it."

While they were cleaning and bandaging my knee, I took advantage of having Mom's full attention to announce, "When I grow up I want to be a grease monkey."

"What's a grease monkey?" Mom wasn't very knowledgeable about cars.

"It's slang for a car mechanic." Mackie knew a lot about cars.

Mom made her opinion clear, "Girl's don't become car mechanics." I was hoping for some support from Mackie, but he never undercut Mom's position as my parent.

But Mom, who was still young, 31 in 1950, did get upset at Mackie while I was around. One day he was late picking me up after school so I decided to walk home. I lost my way a bit but I made it home okay, after all it was only a few blocks from school. Mom was furious at Mackie for not taking better care of me. I was furious that no one appreciated how adventurous and capable I was.

Mackie was picking me up after school because the year I was in first grade I lived with my grandparents during the week. Dad was away at sea as the Engineering Officer on the USS *Rochester,* a navy cruiser. He was helping to fight the Korean War. Mom had her hands full taking care of baby Maggie, toddler Pat, and four-year-old John, my two younger sisters and my brother. Mackie, my grandfather, was retired and he could take me to school and pick me up just as he was taking Gram, my non-driving grandmother, to her job on a factory assembly line and picking her up. I spent weekends with Mom and my siblings.

Mackie was likely involved with my wanting to be a grease monkey, and he definitely helped me on the way to my next ambition. As a first grader at St Mathias Catholic School, I told the world about my goals in a class assignment to write "A Story About When I Grow Up." It began "As far as I know I really want to be an astronomer." I also had another ambition and midway through the story I wrote "When the men who are making the first space ship get finished, I am going to the moon."

My teacher shared my essay with the other nuns. The nun who taught the third or fourth grade class, Sister Mary Joan, asked if I could read it to her class. My teacher, as she was returning my essay, let me know of the request.

"How will I do that?" I asked. "They are in a different classroom."

"This afternoon Sister Mary Joan will send someone to escort you to her classroom so you can read it to them." It sounded like fun. Something different to do.

With my story in front of me, I went off to the big kids' classroom to tell them of my ambitions. When I stood in front of the class one of the students in the back complained, "I can't see her, she's too small."

Sister Mary Joan immediately had a solution. "Stand on this chair, that way the whole class can see you."

When I finished there was a polite round of applause, probably prompted by the teacher who said, "Thank you, Mary, now let's get you back to your classroom."

This was my first public speaking gig and even though none of my audience seemed too interested, I was secretly thrilled. No one had said "Girls don't become astronomers."

I have puzzled about my wanting to go to the moon. Why would I want to do that? This was 1951. The *Apollo 11* moon landing was over 18 years in the future and *Sputnik* wouldn't be launched for another six years. I hadn't yet discovered science fiction, we didn't have a TV, and I doubt that anyone had ever taken me to a Buck Rogers movie. There was nothing in my environment that would lead a small child like me to create by herself the novel idea of going to the moon. What adult could have influenced me? There is no doubt in my mind that my grandfather, Mackie, was that adult. Mackie, a retired businessman, had plenty of time to spend with an inquisitive six-year-old, introducing her to the things of the world, especially new futuristic things. As a forward-looking individual, he opened my mind to new ideas about what the future might be like. He was the only adult in my young life who never told me "girls don't" especially when I began to share his view of the future.

My favorite story about Mackie looking to the future came from Gram. She told me about their first airplane trip after O'Hare Airport opened. Today, O'Hare is one of the busiest airports in the world, but in the beginning it was very quiet. Major airlines were still flying out of Chicago's other airport, Midway. After their first trip departing from O'Hare, my grandmother never wanted to fly out of that airport again because it was so deserted but my grandfather said, "Just wait, this will become an exciting place to be."

Mom frequently talked about Mackie's interest in new and futuristic things by saying something like, "It's a shame Mackie died before computers; he would have loved them."

After I recounted my trip to the big kids' classroom, Mom helped me put together a booklet entitled "Important Things about Astronomy." We cut out articles and pictures from the newspaper and magazines and pasted them onto the pages of the book. I even included a picture of an early spacesuit.

Mackie is the reason I still have my essay on going to the moon. He didn't throw it out and after he died Gram continued to keep it. When she died, Mom discovered it among her things and gave it to me.

***

The summer I turned seven Mom told me that things were about to change. "John is starting kindergarten in the fall," she said, "so I will be able to take both of you to school and you don't have to live with your grandparents during the week anymore."

I'm sure I responded positively. I was an agreeable child, perhaps even a thoughtful child who realized that with four children seven and younger, Mom didn't need anyone to argue with her. The plus about living at home with Mom and my siblings was that I had my brother, John, to play with. And we could play outdoors. My grandparents lived in a third-floor apartment and they were really indoor people. But even as a seven-year-old, I knew what this change would cost me. With four children, each with their own needs, Mom had limited time to pay attention to me. And since I was the oldest Mom wanted me to help take care of the younger children. I had reveled in the attention that my grandparents paid to me while I was living with them. I have lots of memories of the year I was six when I was learning new and exciting things and was encouraged to believe that I could be part of those exciting things. I have no actual memories of the year I was seven.

With John starting kindergarten there were two of us going to St Mathias Catholic School in Chicago. Normally kindergarten was only a half day but the nuns understood the difficulty Mom would have had, picking John up in the middle of the day or dropping him off in the middle of the day, so they let him go to both sessions of the kindergarten class.

The nuns were helpful. One day I arrived at school without my lunch. My teacher was in the process of determining what I wanted for lunch so that she could have the convent kitchen make me a sandwich when a friend of my mother's, who I called Aunt Betty, came to my rescue with a lunch she had made for me.

But the nuns also made mistakes.

One day, when I was in first grade, my teacher told me that only Catholics could go to heaven. I was horrified. My grandparents were not Catholic, and I didn't want them to go to Hell. The nun had also said that Hell was for bad people. That upset me even more because Gram and Mackie were not bad people. That evening I told my grandmother about what I'd learned.

"That is the stupidest thing I've ever heard," Gram exploded. "Of course people other than Catholics go to heaven."

I think my problems with organized religion and their senseless "rules" began that day.

After I moved back with the family, Mom made sure I never took my brother and walked home with him if she was late. Mom's friend "Aunt Betty" lived down the block from the school and two of her children, Roger and Ann, also went to St Mathias. We walked home with them after school and Mom picked us up at their house.

***

Life changed again shortly before I turned eight. Dad came home from sea with orders to his new duty station in Washington, D.C.

With Dad being a career naval officer we had already moved a lot. I was born in 1944 at the Mare Island Naval Hospital in Vallejo, California, but we left when I was a few months old. For the next four years when Dad's ship was in port we lived near naval bases around the country in towns such as Bremerton, Washington; Anacostia, Virginia; Charleston, South Carolina; New London, Connecticut; Brooklyn, New York; and Annapolis, Maryland. We also spent some time in Texas when Dad was trying out the idea of being a navy pilot.

When Dad's ship was at sea during the first four years of my life we returned to Chicago so Mom would not be alone. Since Dad was at sea when John arrived in 1946, he was born at Great Lakes Naval Base near Chicago.

Dad, John, Pat, me, Maggie and Mom—I was six and a half

Then the navy decided that Dad needed a Master of Science degree in Petroleum Engineering and sent him to the University of California at Berkeley. Pat was born in 1949 while we were there. We returned to Chicago shortly before Dad left for Korea. So, just like John, Maggie was born at Great Lakes in 1950. Moving was nothing new.

But this move ended the first time in my life that I'd lived in one place for almost two years. I had gone to school with the same children for those two years, and they were all about to disappear from my life. I don't remember how I felt about that. Today, when someone asks me what it was like to move every few years, my response is "it was normal." Maybe the nomadic living conditions of my early years had already convinced my eight-year-old self that moving and its consequences were normal. Maybe I still had to experience the trauma of leaving behind the friends that I'd known for two years. By the time I was a teenager and had actual memories of moves, I had built a wall to protect myself. I accepted that most people were only in my life for a period of time and then they were gone. Most children grow up with neighbors and family they remember. There was that special person or persons who helped shape their life and the difficult person or persons who never let them forget anything they ever did wrong. My early life was a series of different people passing through, most of whom I don't remember at all.

Mom was happy that Dad was home. She said he was never going to be away at sea again. He had requested a change of designation from Line Officer to Engineering Duty Only Officer. This meant that all his future assignments would be ashore.

I'm sure I was glad to have Dad home again, although after being away for two years, he was probably a bit of a stranger. For me the most exciting thing was that we were leaving our cramped apartment to live in a house with a big yard in Arlington, Virginia.

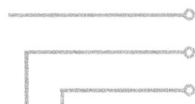

From Coast to Coast

AS PROMISED, THE new house in Arlington had a large back yard. The mulberry tree in the middle of the yard was great to climb but the mulberries stained our clothes which Mom didn't like. There were huckleberry bushes along the back fence. The huckleberry bushes might have been the reason we had fireflies at night. I had never seen fireflies before. They were thinner than normal flies, and their tails lit up from time to time at night. You could catch fireflies in a jar and when many of them were lit up at the same time, it was very bright. We had to make sure we let them out of the jar before they died.

We lived across the street from a retired couple, Mr. and Mrs. B. They had an attic where Mrs. B kept all of the books that had belonged to her brother. He'd owned all the books written by Edgar Rice Burroughs. I started with the Tarzan books and then discovered that Edgar Rice Burroughs had also written books about other characters. I especially enjoyed his books about John Carter of Mars. I was only allowed to read the B's books at their house, but they were nice enough to allow me to spend enough time at their house to read all of their books.

The other great thing that Mr. and Mrs. B had was a TV in their living room. Our whole family was invited over to watch the first Inauguration of President Eisenhower in 1953. I also went over and watched the Pick Temple show in the afternoon. It was like the Howdy Doody show except that children from the Washington, D.C., area could send in their name and possibly be on the show. I got chosen once. I sat at the far end of the top row, and Mom was upset because the TV camera didn't show me often. Being on the show wasn't as exciting as I had thought it would be. You were just watching the show from the back instead from in front.

With Dad home there were now two adults to take care of four children and we started doing family outings. Many of our destinations were Civil War battlefields. Mom was the instigator of these trips. She had gotten interested in the Civil War after reading *House Divided* by Ben Ames Williams. For me the most interesting battlefield was Gettysburg. The rocks to climb and hills to hike made it my favorite. However, I was also aware of the historic nature of that battlefield because it was such a decisive battle during the Civil War.

Mom had always been interested in history and shared her love of historical people and events with me. With Dad being a naval officer, I became interested in the history of the United States Navy. I found biographies of famous people a good way to learn about historical events, and I read about the lives of early naval heroes like John Paul Jones, Oliver Hazard Perry and David Farragut. I liked learning more about these men. After all, they had once been children like me struggling to find their place in the world.

Reading in general, not just reading about history, was an encouraged activity. I got my first library card when we were in Chicago and one of the first things we did after moving was to get new library cards. One clear memory I have of the Virginia years is sitting in a window seat alcove in the library and reading. It was a comfortable spot with a nice deep red paisley cushion on the seat. In addition to history books, I discovered science fiction books while we were in Virginia.

When the people who owned the house we rented returned to Arlington, we had to move to a house in nearby Alexandria. The new townhouse was brick not wood and did not have a yard so there was nothing interesting about it. We only lived there for a year before Dad got orders transferring him to Bremerton, Washington. So the summer I turned eleven we drove across the country to our next home.

***

Even though I'd been across the country multiple times, this was the first cross-country trip I remember. I started on the trip before the rest of the family. Grandma, Dad's mother, had been visiting and when she returned home, I accompanied her on the train back to Chicago. She was visiting by herself as Grandpa, Dad's father, had died the first year we were in Virginia.

We had all gone to his funeral in Park Ridge, the suburb of Chicago, where Grandpa and Grandma lived. Dad and his oldest brother, Uncle Paul, drove from Arlington to Park Ridge so they could be there as soon as possible. Uncle Paul's family, Aunt Charlotte, Paul Jr. and Don, who were also living in Arlington at the time, went on the train with us. My father's middle brother, Uncle Carl, and his family, Aunt Regi, Mike, Kate and Liz, lived in a house across the street from Grandpa and Grandma so they didn't have to travel.

We had spent time with Grandma and Grandpa when we lived in Chicago. But not enough time for me to form a close relationship with either of my paternal grandparents. Grandpa died when I was eight and I have no memories of him. In the only picture ever taken of all of the cousins and their grandparents, it looks like he might be saying something to me. I wonder what it was.

In front: Kate holding Liz, Grandma holding Maggie, Mike and Don
In back: Me, Pat, Grandpa, John, and Paul Jr.

The only memory I have of school while we were in Arlington came after we got back from Grandpa's funeral. I had missed a week of school and the only thing that seemed to be important to my teacher, who was a nun, was that I hadn't done all of the arithmetic problems in my workbook while I was gone. So I had to go out into the hall an hour a day and work on them. This was really silly as I was good at arithmetic and doing extra addition and subtraction problems didn't teach me anything new. I wonder if they were just enforcing the rules or if they were punishing me for not getting caught up as part of my homework.

While I was waiting for the rest of the family to leave Virginia and begin our trip west, I played baseball with my cousin Mike on their front lawn. He was always the Chicago White Sox; I was always the New York Yankees.

When I was pitching to Mike I was Whitey Ford, when I was batting I was Mickey Mantle. I had become interested in baseball and the Yankees were my team. I knew all the famous baseball players on all the teams and all their stats. I may have picked up my interest in baseball from Mackie as he listened to baseball games on the radio. Or it may just have been one of the "boy" things that I got involved with because I found it interesting.

We drove across the country in our Chevy station wagon named "Nancy." Nancy looked like a "woody," a part-steel part-wood car, with its dark green body covered on the side and tailgate by dark faux wood panels trimmed with lighter faux wood. But it was a new and modern all-steel car. This car was actually "Nancy 3." John says that naming our cars Nancy was from a Gilbert and Sullivan song about "...with my Nancy on my knee." The Gilbert and Sullivan operettas were about the only music I remember having in the house when I was a child. But I'm not convinced as my memory is that Gilbert and Sullivan entered our life later than our first car named Nancy which was purchased in 1947 or 1948.

While driving across the county we stopped at interesting places like the Corn Palace, the Badlands, Yellowstone, Craters of the Moon and the fish ladders on the Columbia River near Portland, Oregon. We saw Mount Rushmore and the plans for the Crazy Horse memorial which was just starting to be carved into a mountain. The Corn Palace was interesting as it was covered with murals made from corn and other grains. However, what I really remember about it was that they served ice cold water. It was hot driving across the country in the summer, and our car didn't have air conditioning. In 1955 not many cars did. It was so hot that Mom and Dad would get up early, about 4 a.m., wake up John and me and load the still sleeping younger girls into the car. They would then drive for several hours in the dark to avoid the heat of the day.

One of my favorite pictures from the cross-country trip is me at Craters of the Moon National Monument and Preserve. My interest in eventually going to the moon hadn't waned and everyone kidded me about it. I always knew I would become a scientist but after the trip across country I briefly moved away from the idea of becoming an astronomer and seriously considered becoming a geologist. The different kinds of rocks we discovered on the trip were amazing. There was obsidian, so shiny and sharp; feldspar which Dad said was rock that didn't quite become obsidian; and geodes, rocks which when you broke them open revealed an interior set of beautiful crystals around an empty space. Dad taught me about rocks on the trip across country. He was interested in science and geology was one of his main interests. Dad was always asking questions and trying to learn new things. He once told me that he was sure that at one time Africa and South America were joined together. Today, everyone accepts the theory of plate tectonics and moving continents, but in the mid-1950s this wasn't generally accepted and wasn't what we were taught in school. Dad, however, was sure that someday things would change and everyone would understand, like he did, that at one time South America and Africa were connected.

"Mary on the Moon"–
in Craters of the Moon National Monument and Preserve

The trip across country solidified Dad as an important person in my life. Even though he'd had a shore job the three years we were in Virginia, he was working long hours and making trips to Europe. Still, during that time, he had encouraged my growing interest in doing things outdoors and he often led the expeditions climbing up the hills at Gettysburg or tromping around other battlefields. But on the trip across country, he had time to talk to me and enjoyed talking to me about scientific things. In those days I was a sponge, soaking up whatever new information anyone was willing to share with me. Both my parents enjoyed talking about what they knew, a trait I now share. And for me it was a way to have my parents pay attention to me.

About this time, my soaking up information started to morph into a new skill. I remember a question my teacher asked during a history class in fifth or sixth grade. It wasn't a fair question. She hadn't yet told us the answer and we were not expected to have ideas of our own.

"How would our life have been different if the Persians had defeated the Greeks?"

I was stunned. I knew the answer even if no one had ever told me what the answer was. My hand went up and I blurted out my answer.

"We wouldn't have had a democracy."

"Yes, Mary," my teacher replied.

She then explained to the class about how the democracy of the Greeks would have been snuffed out by the autocratic Persians. And without the legacy of Greek democracy, we might not have ended up with our democratic form of government. Until that moment, it had never occurred to me that I could put two pieces of knowledge together to create a new idea. It was a skill I would need to become a scientist.

Neither of my parents ever said "girls don't think" or even "girls don't learn" and encouraged me to do both of those things. But in their hearts they were traditionalists. And encouragement to learn was not the same as encouragement to have a career. It was a shame that Mom didn't inherit

Mackie's non-traditional view of the world. After all, with Dad being gone so often and with all of our moves, Mom was the only consistent adult in my young life. I might not have been any more driven to follow my dreams if she had encouraged me to do what I wanted but I probably would have been imbued with more confidence.

***

As usual, when we reached our next duty station, the navy's support for the newly arrived adults kicked in. Our first house in Bremerton, on Gregory Way, was waiting for us. It belonged to the parents of one of Dad's Naval Academy classmates. There was a "Welcome Aboard" party for the adults at the Officers' Club shortly after we arrived so that Mom and Dad could meet other military in the area. We kids were on our own until school started and we could make friends there. John and I spent the rest of the summer exploring our new town. As I was eleven and he was almost nine, we had the freedom to go out by ourselves. The town was small enough we could walk downtown and many times stopped for a soda at the drug store. Sometimes we could afford to splurge on a milkshake.

Bremerton

WE ONLY LIVED on Gregory Way for a few months. The house was too small so we moved to a bigger house on Taft Avenue. I thought it was a great house but Dad didn't like it. His objection was that the house never warmed up in the winter. The house came with a dark gray cat that Dad named "Cassius." I think he named him Cassius because he was a fat cat, and it was a joke about a line in Shakespeare's *Julius Caesar* where Caesar makes a comment about Cassius having a lean and hungry look. Dad liked puns a lot. They were his favorite type of joke. The thing I liked best about the Taft house was that it was on the water, and I could go for long walks on the beach or in the woods between the houses and the beach. Our lot was covered with tall trees I could shimmy up and disappear. We also had a huge apple tree out front that I could climb in. My parents didn't specifically tell me that "girls don't climb trees," but I was periodically reminded that climbing trees was not very feminine. Playing soccer with John in our front yard wasn't very feminine either.

Dad finally got his way and we moved to our third Bremerton house on Burwell Street. It was on a small lot and closer to school. The most interesting things about the yard were the pear tree, the trellis with grapes growing on it and the blackberry bushes by the garage. Great fruit for snacking.

While in Bremerton our family outings expanded to multiday trips as we started camping. At first we camped in the car like we had sometimes on the trip across country. Maggie slept in the front seat. John slept in the second seat. Mom, Dad, Pat and I slept in the back area of the station wagon with our feet on the open tail gate. It was crowded and at first we fit. But we were all getting bigger and so it became too crowded. Mom and Dad got a tent for us. The tent was hard to put up but it was real camping in the outdoors.

One of our favorite places to go was Mount Rainier. At over 14,000 feet, the snowcapped inactive volcano towered over the southeastern skyline. It didn't snow in Bremerton, unlike Chicago and Virginia. But we could go to Mount Rainier and there was plenty of snow. We didn't really ski, but we could slide down grooves that we could find or make in snowbanks. We called it "foot skiing." Dad and I talked about hiking the one-hundred-mile Wonderland Trail that goes all the way around Mount Rainier, but we never even did part of it. While Dad enjoyed talking to me about the Wonderland Trail, his priorities were his job, family outings, work for the church and an occasional fishing trip with other men. That didn't leave any time for a multiday hiking trip with me.

"Foot skiing" on Mount Rainier

The camping trips during our Bremerton stay enhanced my interest in outdoor activities. Even the trip to Whidbey Island, where it rained the entire week we were there, didn't dampen my enthusiasm for being outside. Other memorable trips were to Cle Elum where I went on my first trail ride on a horse and to a small lake near home where I discovered that freshly caught trout for breakfast made an excellent meal. One of the rules, in my family, of catching a fish was that you had to clean it. I used this chore to create a project for Freshman

Biology on the contents of fish stomachs. The most interesting fish was the one with a completely empty stomach. It should have waited a little longer before breaking its fast with my fly. Freshman Biology was my first real science class. Most of what was taught in grade school was more basic than what I'd learned from Dad or from reading. I thoroughly enjoyed the class and had no problem with what was considered its most difficult task—dissecting a frog. It was a lot like cleaning a fish.

The first Christmas we were in Bremerton, Gram and Mackie gave me a space station set. It had spaceships and men in spacesuits and different kinds of aliens. I had always been a daydreamer and had invented lots of people to daydream about. But once I got the space set, I started inventing people who lived in space and on other planets. One set of characters I invented lived in the red spot on the planet Jupiter. With our knowledge today of Jupiter's gaseous atmosphere this was clearly impossible but we didn't know much about the planets then. I remember reading a science fiction novel by Robert Heinlein, *Between Planets*, where Venus was a jungle world. We hadn't yet discovered the searing heat and poisonous atmosphere of that planet.

When I was twelve, I succumbed to Mom's opinion that daydreaming was nonproductive and turned my imaginary characters into a novel about the people who lived on Jupiter and the war they fought against the invaders from Earth. At fifteen, I decided that the story was too childish and threw it away. I wish I'd given it to Gram or Mackie for safekeeping as it would be fun to reread it as an adult.

Again I attended a Catholic school in Bremerton. My frustration with the silly rules imposed on me was growing. It was the list of things that "girls did" that bothered me the most. Girls sang in the choir, girls marched in the May Day parade and girls took sewing lessons. I wasn't interested in doing any of these things. Then, when I was fourteen, fate gave me a chance to break loose. Bremerton was a small town and after I graduated from grade school going to a Catholic high school meant taking a ferry every day to Seattle. It was about a one hour trip each way. So I made a request.

"I want to spend my freshman year at West Bremerton High School."

My request was granted. My parents probably thought of it as a practical decision that they had made. Going to Seattle would have been a long trip for me to make every day and it would cost them a lot more than sending me to a Catholic grade school had. With a fifth child on the way, they were probably looking for ways to save money.

For me, it was a step on my way to independence and so at the age of fourteen, after eight years in Catholic schools, I finally got to go to a public school. If I hadn't asked, they probably would have sent me to the Catholic high school in Seattle. Dad, who was born Catholic, felt strongly that we should be educated in our religion. He even taught CCD (Confraternity of Catholic Doctrine) classes for Catholic children who went to public schools. Mom, who converted to Catholicism when she married Dad, didn't feel so strongly about religious education. But I never saw her argue with

Dad about it. Mom always tried to find the middle ground in any disagreement, and she believed that parents shouldn't argue in front of their children. On very rare occasions she would feel strongly about something and express her opinions openly. Religion was not one of those topics.

Once I started high school, I got interested in team sports. Of course, I had been interested in major league baseball for a while, but I never went to an actual game. West Bremerton High School had a football team and I went to all the Friday night home games. There weren't many opportunities for girls to play sports, but I did enjoy playing basketball during PE classes. And the school had a girls' tennis team so I joined that. I wasn't good enough to play in any matches but at least I was on a team. And being on a team meant you could play a sport at a higher level and be pushed by others who wanted to be good at a sport. Being pushed to be better was good for me.

I wasn't pushed academically. I had the kind of smarts that does well in school. It helped ease the transition to a new school. I learned early that being smart got me noticed. But I also learned not to be the smartest kid in the class. Being too smart made it harder to make friends.

When I was in seventh grade I learned that school smarts were not the only type of intelligence there was. I was early to school one morning. Instead of my classroom being full of students moving slowly towards their desks, there were only a few classmates in the room. Everyone was standing around Larry's desk. I didn't know Larry well. With my tenure in any school being short, I tended to make friends with people I thought I'd get along with best and most of them tended to be in the "smart student" group. Larry wasn't in that group. But I was curious about what was going on and joined the crowd around Larry.

What I saw was fascinating. Larry had a plastic engineering template in his hand and was using it to create a pencil drawing of the cockpit dashboard of a spaceship. He was just finishing up one drawing when I arrived. He saw the interest in my face.

"Would you like one?" he asked with a smile.

I nodded and then stood there in awe as, armed only with a pencil and a piece of green plastic, Larry turned a small blank piece of paper into the spaceship cockpit that I had visions of sitting at one day. It was perfect; the edges were nicely curved, no straight lines. The gauges were circles with either lines or numbers in them. Small circles represented the warning lights that were prepared to flash a danger signal. There was a balance to the layout that made it pleasing to look at. I was watching someone display, quite unabashedly, not only technical knowledge but also artistic skill. He was finishing up my drawing as the teacher came into the room and ordered us all to our seats.

"Thank you," I said as Larry handed me the drawing with another smile.

With my gift in hand, I made my way to my own desk on the other side of the room. With the class starting, I had no time to reflect on what had just happened. But later the awe I had felt at Larry's accomplishment was replaced by confusion. It made no sense that someone who could produce such beautiful work was not considered smart.

***

In many ways the most important thing that happened while we were in Bremerton was that we became a family of seven. My brother Dan was born a month and a half after I turned fourteen. It was a bit of a surprise as Maggie, the youngest up until then, was almost eight when Dan was born. I don't remember any of my other siblings as babies so Dan was a new experience. John, Pat, Maggie and I all helped take care of him. He was also fun to play with. I felt very grown-up taking care of the baby.

We had had a nice time in Bremerton, but it was time to move again. Four years in one place was a long time for us. Dad got orders to move to San Francisco and so as I turned fifteen, we were making plans to move again. I wondered if I would enjoy living in a big city and worried that I would hate it. I'd become very fond of my time outdoors.

San Francisco

SAN FRANCISCO WAS home to several Catholic high schools. So I could have easily been sent back to a Catholic school. Fortunately my grades hadn't deteriorated during my year in public high school and I was allowed to attend George Washington High School, the local public high school. Dad's grades had deteriorated when he left the discipline of a Catholic grade school and went to a public high school. My parents were worried about the same thing happening to me. It helped that Washington was ranked nationally as a top high school and, more important to me, it offered a greater variety of science classes than the Catholic high school for girls. John spent eighth grade at Saint Monica Catholic grade school and then went to Saint Ignatius Catholic High School, a boys-only school. He told me later that part of the reason he went to Saint Ignatius was that I was a tough act to follow in school. I was surprised. I knew I was better in math than he was, but always thought he was better than me in other subjects like English. Apparently not.

My youngest brother Chris joined the family in March 1960. For years we had been a family with four children. Then quickly we became a family with six children as Chris arrived less than two years after Dan. John and I referred to Dan and Chris as "the mistake" and "the companion to the mistake." Pat and Maggie were still too young to understand what we were talking about.

Chris and Dan in San Francisco

Dan had been a caesarian baby and Mom's doctor wanted her to have Chris as a caesarian baby as well. So surgery was scheduled. I called from a pay phone at school during my lunch break on the scheduled day to find out that I had a baby brother. Both mother and baby were doing fine.

As frequently happens between teenage girls and their mothers, my relationship with Mom deteriorated while we were in San Francisco. She became uninteresting. Having two little children and temporary health problems may have been a major factor. She expected me to help her take care of the other children, but the responsible eldest daughter wasn't what I wanted to be. However, Dad had more time to spend with me when we lived in San Francisco. He wasn't traveling to Europe and the Middle East like he had when we lived in Virginia, and he and Mom weren't as involved in community activities as they had been in Bremerton. Dad taught me to play chess and encouraged my growing interest in mathematics. One day in class my math teacher told us that it was impossible to develop a formula to create prime numbers. I took this as a challenge. After working on it for several weeks, I was sure I'd created the "impossible" formula. I showed it to Dad. His response was pensive.

"Hmm, I always thought what your teacher said was correct. Let me look at what you've done."

A few days later he gently pointed out the error in my formula. I could have continued to work on the formula, but decided that if both Dad and my math teacher had said that the formula was impossible, maybe I would believe them.

The high school I went to had a chess club and I joined. There were citywide high school chess matches, but I wasn't good enough to compete. I tried once and lost badly. I continued to play with Dad and other chess club members, but I never became good enough to compete at the city level. While I didn't like losing I knew that playing with better players, such as Dad, helped improve my game even if it meant I lost more often than I would like. But losing badly, like I did in the citywide tournament, was pointless.

While Dad encouraged me to learn, he wasn't supportive of my ambition to have a career. One time I asked Dad why he spent so much time teaching me things and why he was planning to send me to college if I wasn't going to use what I learned.

There was surprise in his voice when he replied, as if his answer should have been obvious. "So you can teach your children."

With Mackie's death in February 1960, I lost all family support for being a career woman. Officially Mackie died of a stroke, but he had been different on his last visit shortly after we moved to San Francisco. Instead of being everyone's favorite grandfather, he became critical of everything everyone was doing. It was so unlike him. There must have been something going on even then. It wasn't like he died young as Mackie lived to be eighty-six. However, he probably thought he died young as he always talked about living to be one hundred. Gram was his second wife and was much younger than Mackie, being only sixty-four when he died. Only Dad went back to Chicago for the funeral. Mom was pregnant with Chris and was recovering from encephalitis and decided not to go. She was very close to Mackie so it was a hard decision for her to make.

Dan with Mackie and Gram on Mackie's last visit to San Francisco

In spite of the lack of family support I still continued to look forward to a career after college. In my freshman year in high school I still wanted to be an astronomer. Then I decided to become a nuclear physicist. When I mentioned this new goal to our high school career counselor, she curtly dismissed my dream.

"Do you have any idea what a nuclear physicist does?"

She was correct at one level: I wasn't sure what a nuclear physicist did. But the U. S. Navy had recently acquired nuclear-powered submarines and I was sure that the spaceships that took us to the moon would be nuclear powered. I ignored the unspoken rebuke that girls didn't become nuclear physicists and took a course in physics my junior year instead of waiting, as most students did, until their senior year.

Even though there weren't as many outdoor activities in San Francisco as there had been in Bremerton, I still was able to walk a lot. It was a good city to walk in and, since it had an extensive inexpensive public transit system, when I got tired, I could just catch a bus home. Additionally, the state of California required physical education classes for all students in high school. These classes included team sports for girls. I excelled in baseball and basketball. I had started playing basketball in Bremerton and the summer we moved to San Francisco, John and I entertained ourselves playing baseball. While my parents were looking for a house to buy in San Francisco, we lived in a Quonset hut at Hunter's Point Naval Shipyard. Quonset huts were lightweight, prefabricated structures made of corrugated steel. They resembled a tin can cut in half from top to bottom and laid on its side perched on low concrete blocks. They had been built as temporary housing during World War II. John and I solved the problem of no friends in this new place by playing baseball. We took turns pitching and hitting. Whoever was the batter had to hit the ball and hit it in a controlled fashion. Otherwise the ball would roll under a Quonset hut and be lost. As a result when I started school I was prepared to be a great hitter on my softball team.

Another change when we moved to San Francisco was going to school with a significant number of non-white students. Half of George Washington's students were white.

About a third were black and the rest were Asian. There had been a non-white student or two in one or more of my earlier schools, but this was different. Someone asked me recently how I felt about going to a racially integrated school. I didn't really feel anything about it. Every place we went there was something new, and this was one of the new things about San Francisco. The non-white students I spent the most time with were the other girls on the basketball team. Most of the really good basketball players belonged to various Asian citywide basketball teams.

I got interested in politics and elections while we were in San Francisco. I had watched the Eisenhower inauguration when we were in Virginia but after that, presidents and politics seemed like things unrelated to my life. That changed with the 1960 election. For the first time people were talking seriously about having a Catholic president. I stayed up late the night of the Democratic convention in the summer of 1960, tabulating the votes on a pad of paper until finally Wyoming put John Kennedy over the top. If I had been old enough to vote, I think I would have voted for Richard Nixon based on the issues but it was exciting to finally have a Catholic president.

The summer I turned seventeen turned out to be different than what I was expecting when it began. In mid-May at the end of my junior year in high school, I was selected to be a member of an organization called the Girl's Service Society. It was an honor to be selected, and I wasn't expecting to be chosen. But I was. I hadn't really fit in well at the school. I had friends at school but none of these friendships extended to doing activities outside of school. And while I enjoyed the sports-oriented PE program that was in effect in California in those days, I was more of a starter than a star. But I did well academically, earning mostly A's. That academic prowess was probably the reason for my selection.

So in mid-May 1961, I was on top of the world, having been chosen to be a member of the Girl's Service Society. Shortly thereafter I came crashing back to earth when Dad came home to announce that he was being transferred and we were moving again. It wasn't fair. This was supposed to be a three-year tour of duty, and I would be able to finish high school without moving and having to start all over again at a new school.

I thought about lobbying to stay in San Francisco so I could finish high school, but Dad's orders were to Pearl Harbor so I decided not to fight it. Going to Hawaii had too much appeal.

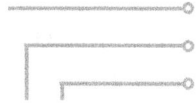

Honolulu

WE SAILED ACROSS the Pacific on a navy transport ship. The cabins were small but functional. And everything was painted steel gray. There were troops on the ship as well but they were kept segregated from us. Some of those troops may have been destined for Vietnam as by 1961 our troop buildup was slowly beginning. It took five days to make the trip. The first day was rough sailing as the continental shelf caused large waves in the ocean. After that the ocean was smooth. It wasn't a boring trip. Among other things, I was part of a group that discovered the control room for the music that played throughout the ship. It was fun being able to decide what music to play. For days we sailed on an inky blue ocean. As we approached Honolulu, there was a sudden change as the ship passed over the edge of the submerged part of the island. The sea became a light blue green.

For the first time we had permanent navy housing. Our house was open and airy as were most houses in Hawaii. And we had a banana grove in the backyard. In nature, each banana tree in the grove would produce one cluster of bananas and then die. But we didn't let them die naturally. Instead, when the first banana on a tree turned yellow, we would cut down the tree and hang its three-to-four-feet mostly green cluster of fruit in the carport. The bananas ripened slowly and so provided a steady supply of fruit that could easily be picked from the cluster. Our house was in the Makalapa housing area on a hill above Pearl Harbor. The local public high school had a terrible reputation so John and I were sent to Maryknoll High School in Honolulu.

I wasn't happy about going back to a Catholic school but the Maryknoll nuns were different from the nuns I'd had in grade school. Maybe because they were a missionary order, they were more worldly and less rule bound. Still, it was back to school uniforms and a limited curriculum. There was no science class I could take. Maryknoll taught physics and chemistry in alternate years and I was there in a physics year, but I'd taken that in San Francisco my junior year. I ended up with a study hall for the first time in my high school career because there was no class available for me to take that period. That only lasted one semester as in my second semester I was able to take part two of mechanical drawing. I'd taken the first semester in San Francisco.

I wasn't allowed to participate in the one expansion of the curriculum. All the boys at Maryknoll High School became members of the Civil Air Patrol and could learn how to fly. John had no interest in flying and I was jealous because I would have loved to learn how to fly. After all, the astronauts in Project Mercury, our first manned space program, were all pilots. I was never angry at John because he happened to have been born a boy and thus had opportunities I didn't have. He had his own problems with the culture in which we were raised. In contrast to me, of whom nothing was expected, everything was expected of him as the oldest son. It was important that he have a successful career and marry well as his job was to maintain the honor of the family in the future. Plus, with the addition of the two younger boys, he had to be a role model for them.

Dad taught John to drive a car in Hawaii as he had taught me to drive in San Francisco. The trend would continue as Dad would teach Pat to drive in Virginia, our next duty station. For some reason, he was unable to teach Maggie to drive and so that job would fall to me. I didn't get to drive much in San Francisco. The car was always in use. Dad drove to work every day and when we went on family trips to places like Yosemite and Mount Lassen, he also drove. I really started driving in Hawaii. Unlike San Francisco it wasn't a place where you could get around on foot or by bus. We bought a second car, a Volkswagen Beetle, soon after we moved to Hawaii, and Mom was delighted to have another driver in the family who could run errands. I didn't tell her about the time I packed the whole tennis team into the car.

The racial makeup at Maryknoll was interesting. Whites or "haoles," to use the Hawaiian word, were in the minority. Most of my friends were of either Chinese or Filipino descent. My date for the senior prom, Zac, was Filipino and Mom was glad that the prom was early enough that Gram, who came for my graduation, didn't meet him. After all Gram had said that the only problem with Dad, who was of German descent, was that he wasn't English. No one was sure how she would respond to one of her grandchildren dating an Asian person. The other benefit of having friends with a different ethnic background was that I was introduced to a variety of new foods. An important discovery was that vegetables didn't need to be cooked in the British style of green mush.

I thoroughly enjoyed my year at Maryknoll. Even though I was new, I fit into my class easily. It might have been that it was a small school. Unlike Washington High School where I was part of a class of six hundred students, my Maryknoll graduating class had less than a hundred students. So I knew everyone in my class, even if not well. And with John being a sophomore, I knew most of the sophomore class as well.

My sporting activities continued in Hawaii. I acquired some skill as a surfer. But my main sport was tennis. My tennis game had improved and I was good enough to be the top singles player on the team. Unfortunately, we had a weak girls' tennis team and lost every inter-school match we played. Still, I received my "letter" in tennis and won several trophies during Maryknoll-only tournaments.

I continued to excel academically and was a member of the National Honor Society. As part of that organization, I was able to organize tutoring for weaker students. I was the math tutor. I also followed in my parents' footsteps and worked on our high school yearbook. Well, almost in their footsteps, Dad worked on his college yearbook, not his high school one.

***

It seemed as I grew older, that people started using the phrase "girls don't" more frequently. For a while no one talked much about my ambition to become a scientist, but eventually I understood that girls didn't become scientists any more than they became car mechanics. Girls mostly became wives and mothers. If they had a job first, they became teachers or nurses. They certainly didn't become naval officers or engineers like Dad. Secretly I would have loved to have followed in Dad's footsteps, but he didn't approve of women in the military. This was different than his lack of support for my having a career. It wasn't a matter of tradition; he was personally opposed to women in the military. However, one of the reasons Robert Heinlein's *Starship Troopers* was my favorite science fiction novel was that it had women naval officers in it and some of them even commanded starships.

Eventually, I came up with an idea that seemed to work. Becoming a doctor, or more specifically a pediatrician because they worked with children, might be something that girls could do. So by my senior year in high school, I had decided to become a doctor.

My first choice for college had been Georgetown University. It had the premier Catholic medical school in the country and as soon as I decided I was going to be a doctor, I put Georgetown at the top of my list. After attending three high schools I was determined to go to only one college. Much to my dismay, I discovered that Georgetown didn't accept women into their liberal arts program. It was for men only. In those days university premed programs were taught in their College of Liberal Arts. I could have gone to Georgetown's College of Nursing, but just because all the girls I knew were going to become nurses, teachers or social workers didn't mean I had to. So I picked Marquette University in Milwaukee, Wisconsin, which had the second or third best Catholic medical school in the country. And I spent all four years of college there. A big factor in choosing Marquette was that I wanted to go to college on the mainland. My parents insisted that I pick a college somewhere near Chicago so I would have family nearby. Marquette worked out well. With Milwaukee being over an hour from Chicago, I was close enough for family visits and far enough away that I wasn't under family scrutiny all the time.

***

When I graduated from high school my parents gave me a choice of a ten-day trip to Japan or contact lenses as a graduation present. I really wanted contact lenses, having worn glasses since I was about eleven. I needed glasses sooner than that but refused to admit it until I could no longer see the blackboard even when sitting in the front row of the classroom. However, there was no way I was going to turn down a trip to Japan. The reason that the two potential gifts were about the same price was that Dad could take me "space available" on a military flight going to Japan. It made our travel plans a little iffy as we had to wait until there were empty seats on a plane going our way, but it was free. As it turned out, you could get contact lenses in Japan for less than $20 so I ended up getting both gifts.

In the 1960s many things in Japan were inexpensive. I used my graduation money to buy both a camera and a typewriter for school. If I'd bought them in Hawaii, I would have had to decide which one to get.

Dad and I talked about climbing Mount Fuji but our trip ended before the hiking season on Mount Fuji opened. We spent time in Tokyo, Kyoto and the Miyanoshita area. Kyoto was the historic capital of Japan and retained much of the old architecture in its buildings. Miyanoshita was in a rural area with great hiking trails and a large lake with boat tours. On one of our hikes we came across a restaurant with a sign out front announcing the type of establishment as it would have been pronounced by the Japanese "lestaurant." Knowing that no one would believe us, we took a picture. Except in tourist areas there weren't many signs in English and few Japanese spoke English. Dad spoke a little Japanese leftover from his days in World War II. But we got by. Pointing at things worked well. One time I was trying to copy the Japanese character for Coca Cola from the bottle of Coke I was drinking. Our waitress was amused at my attempts. So I handed her my notebook and pencil and she wrote the character for me. Having the correctly written character for Coke turned out to be useful when we were in the countryside and no one spoke any English.

***

The other thing of note from my year in Hawaii was that I got a real tan. It wasn't obvious how dark I had gotten as with my blonde hair, blue eyes and fair skin I still looked lighter than everyone else. However, two pictures taken about a week apart illustrate the change Hawaii had had on me. The first was taken before I left Hawaii to go away to college. I'm the pale one surrounded by my Hawaiian friends. Then I had a reunion in San Francisco with my friends from sophomore and junior year. I'm the dark one surrounded by my California friends.

I'm the light one in the front

I'm the dark one in the back

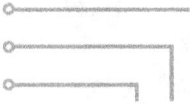

College

I LEFT HAWAII in August 1962 so I could spend some time in Chicago to shop for clothes before starting school. I had nothing to wear in cold weather. Gram helped me pick out a wardrobe suitable for a college freshman in the Midwest.

There was a special benefit for children of military personnel in Hawaii going to school on the mainland. Twice a year a free trip between Hickam Air Force Base near Honolulu and Travis Air Force Base near San Francisco was provided on a space-available basis so I could go to college in the fall and come home in the summer. I spent Christmases with my grandmothers while the family lived in Hawaii. Mom and Dad had no money to bring me home for Christmas. I had to allow extra time getting between California and Chicago as I had to take the train because it was cheaper than flying. But the lack of money was just another thing to live with as Dad never made much money being in the military.

Staying with Grandma, Dad's mother, at Christmas time had an unexpected benefit. I got to know Dad's brother Uncle Carl well. He gave me my first alcoholic drink—a martini. I hated it. I enjoyed talking to him. He reminded me a lot of Dad without the rigidness. One Christmas Uncle Carl announced that he didn't want presents. He had everything he needed except for cashmere socks. He seemed surprised when everyone gave him a pair or two of cashmere socks.

I got my first job when I started college. I had a scholarship and Mom and Dad gave me as much money as they could spare, but it wasn't enough. To come up with the rest of the money, I got a job working at the university library. I did several different things at the library but my favorite job was "shelving," putting returned books back on the shelves. Because I was working in different areas of the library, books that I would never have noticed passed through my hands. As a result I read some interesting books on subjects new to me. I was the only one in my dorm area that had to work. But when the group had pizza and sodas in the evening, they always saved some for me to eat when I got back from working at the library.

I was to have another summer and a half in Hawaii as Dad didn't get transferred to Washington, D. C., until the summer after my sophomore year in college. As that was my last summer in Hawaii you would think I would have spent it on the beach, but I spent much of it in the pool trying to log fifty miles, a quarter of a mile at a time. I was not a good swimmer. The athletic Kennedy administration was always setting up athletic challenges for the country. This was one of them.

Mom and I also made a trip to Kauai. I'd missed the family trip to the "Big Island" of Hawaii as I'd been away at college.

***

After all my earlier complaints about Catholic schools, it might seem strange that I would choose a Catholic college. But my year at Maryknoll High School in Hawaii had erased most of my concerns about Catholic schools. The senseless rules, for the most part, disappeared and the nuns seemed to be okay with our exploring ideas outside of the Catholic mainstream. We weren't permitted to stay outside of ortho-dox belief but looking around and asking questions was acceptable. One of my teachers, Sister Neri or Sister Ana, probably suggested Marquette as a college I might attend.

Marquette was a Jesuit college. The Jesuits have a rep-utation in some circles that almost borders on heresy. Still, Catholic students were required to take five theology class-es. These classes were a long way from the rigid catechism classes I'd had in grade school. We looked at other religions and at the historical implications of religions. We studied older established theologians like Thomas Aquinas who was affectionately referred to by students as "good old TA." We were also introduced to newer theological thinkers like Teilhard de Chardin. It was a thinking encouraged environment.

Most premed students were majoring in biology or chemistry, but I decided to major in mathematics. I took math every semester I was in college even though it wasn't required as part of the premed program. College mathematics wasn't as intuitively obvious as my high school classes had been, but it was still a subject I was good at.

In spite of getting my degree in math, my interest in history never waned. I took a lot of history classes in college. Because of Mom's encouragement, my historical knowledge was much greater than that of the average high school graduate. I took a test before college started that allowed me to skip the first semester of world history. College expanded my knowledge as I had to choose classes that were available, not necessarily classes about times I was interested in. One of the classes I stumbled into, because it fit into my schedule, and thoroughly enjoyed was American Diplomatic History. Most history classes taught what happened. This class provided more information about *why* things happened. I did consider getting a degree in history but that would have been a Bachelor of Arts degree which required two semesters of speech classes. By getting a Bachelor of Science in mathematics I only had to take one speech class. Back in those days standing up and speaking before a group of people was hard for me to do.

An unexpected impact of focusing on Bachelor of Science topics rather than Bachelor of Arts topics was that I stopped writing while I was in college. For a long time I had thought of myself as a writer. After writing my first novel when I was twelve and throwing it away when I was fifteen, I wrote short stories and poetry. I did well enough on writing assignments in high school that sometimes teachers read my efforts to the class, and it was a rare thing for teachers to read students' efforts to a class. During college everyone I knew was writing lots of papers. I wrote only two in the four years I was at Marquette. The first paper was written in my freshman year in Introductory English Composition and my second was written my senior year when I took an anthropology class because I'd run out of required courses to take. Even the history classes I took didn't require that I write anything. I didn't miss writing. I had plenty of other work to do. And after all I was a technical person. I really didn't need to write. But part of me was sad to see some of who I was going away.

On the other hand I developed new interests as I discovered art on trips to Chicago. I had started college not planning to go to Chicago unless I had to, but I quickly realized Chicago was much more interesting than Milwaukee. Sometimes my roommate Joanne joined me on these trips. It was on one of those trips that we went to the Art Institute of Chicago. I had met Joanne my freshman year as like me she was in the premed program. She was also an artist. After I took her to the Rosenwald Museum of Science and Industry, she took me to the Art Institute of Chicago. At first I was unimpressed. Then halfway across a room I turned around for some reason and saw Monet's *Water Lilies* in a whole new way. They looked so different from a distance than they did up close. Clearly there was something new here that I needed to understand. Why would your distance from a painting make a difference in what it looked like?

It was easy to take the train between Milwaukee and Chicago, and Gram was happy to put me up for the weekend. In one of his letters, Dad complained about my not spending more time with his mother. In my letters home, I reported on what I was doing, including trips to Chicago. I told him that I would do better. But I didn't. It was easier to get to Gram's and she was much more interesting than Grandma. It might have been an age thing. Gram was nine years younger than Grandma and the late sixties can be a lot younger than the late seventies. But there was more to it than that. Dad got his "traditional" view of the world from Grandma. While she had convinced my grandfather that they should send their sons to college, she saw no reason for a girl to go to college. And she found my nontraditional goal of having a career incomprehensible. On the other hand, Gram's "girls don't" admonitions were mostly related to finding a husband.

"Men don't want a wife who is smarter than they are," she would say. "You have to defer to them and support their ambitions."

But she thought my going to college was fine and regretted that they hadn't been able to afford to send Mom to four years of college so she could have gotten her degree. Gram also enjoyed shopping, movies and card playing, activities that seemed unimportant to Grandma.

Still, one of the great regrets in my life is that I didn't get to know Grandma better. That regret comes from a picture. All of the memories that I have of Grandma are of an unsmiling severe-looking woman. Most of the pictures that we have of her reflect these memories. But the one picture that doesn't is remarkable. It is a picture of a young woman dressed in a native Algerian costume. You can tell the outfit is colorful, even though it is a black and white photograph, and you certainly wouldn't expect the prim matron that I knew to be wearing pants. All I know about the events surrounding the photograph is that my grandmother worked for a while as a cook in a hotel in Algeria. No one seems to know anymore why or when she was in Algeria. We don't know if she learned to cook before or after her stay there, but do I remember Grandma being a really good cook even if she couldn't get me to eat red cabbage or sauerkraut. All of her grandchildren fondly remember the cookies she made. And now there is no way to hear the stories she had to tell of her life before she became the prim matron I remember.

Grandma in Algeria

The other reason for going to Chicago was that cigarettes were cheaper there than they were in Milwaukee. Like many others, I took up smoking when I went to college. Some of my classmates in high school had smoked, but I didn't have any interest in smoking then. The interesting thing was that as soon as I started to run out of money each month, something that happened most months, the first thing I stopped spending money on was cigarettes. It finally occurred to me that if I stopped smoking I wouldn't run out of money so fast, so I stopped smoking. This made me unusual as almost all adults smoked in those days

The closest friend I made in college was Joanne. Both of us had trouble with the assigned roommates we had our freshman year and after a second roommate not working out during the first semester of our sophomore year, we decided to try rooming together. We were both worried that it would hurt our friendship as clearly neither of us was great room-mate material. But it turned out fine. Since Dad had roomed with other midshipmen at the Naval Academy, I talked to him about the problems I was having getting along with roommates and he told me it would work out. That learning to live with roommates in college was good training for life. He said that the experiences I was having would help me when it came time to have a permanent roommate. He also said that his "permanent roommate" agreed with him on this. I knew he was talking about Mom who had lived at home during her college career.

Joanne had another advantage as a roommate. She had a record player and an extensive record collection. I'd had to leave all of my music behind when I went to college as the only record player in the house belonged to the whole family. Joanne's family provided her with enough money to keep expanding her record collection. She was happy to share her music with me.

In early 1964 we gathered with others in the dorm's TV room to see the debut of the Beatles on the Ed Sullivan show At first everyone was laughing at how silly they looked with their long, shaggy haircuts. Then their music reached us and the room got quiet as everyone listened. The record collection quickly expanded to include Beatle records. Our first purchases included the songs played on the Ed Sullivan show like "All My Loving" and "I Want To Hold Your Hand." We became such Beatles fans that we saw their first movie, *A Hard Day's Night,* more than ten times.

***

Two family members died while I was in college. Grandma died the June after my sophomore year. She had had her first heart attack on one of my visits to Chicago when I was staying with her. I got up late, which was normal and was something that Grandma didn't approve of. That day she was still in her bathrobe with her hair hanging down when I got up. For my active, always properly dressed grandmother to be lying on the couch in her bedclothes at that late hour of the day really scared me. I had never seen her hair down before. Fortunately I had the sense to call my Aunt Regi who still lived across the street. Grandma was unsuccessful in convincing Aunt Regi that it was just indigestion and that she would be fine. Aunt Regi called for an ambulance and I was assigned the task of riding in the ambulance with Grandma to the hospital. My nervousness must have been obvious as Grandma started talking.

"Did I ever tell you about the only time I've been to the hospital?" she asked.

I said something non-committal and Grandma continued the story.

"It was on my first date with your Grandpa. I hurt my leg getting off of the streetcar, and he had to take me to the hospital."

I'd heard the story before but this time it was much more poignant.

I'd already gone home for the summer before I knew how sick Grandma was. Dad did go back to Chicago before she died as it was obvious that her heart was failing. He came home before the funeral to attend John's graduation from high school.

The second death that year was on Mom's side of the family. Gram's older sister, my Aunt Peg, died in the fall of my junior year. I went down to Chicago for the funeral. It was the first wake that I had ever attended, and I was initially surprised at how cheerful everyone was. But then I realized that everyone was just remembering Aunt Peg fondly. I had gotten to know her well enough while I was in college to have memories to share. A favorite memory was the start of my card-playing career. Every Sunday Gram would take the bus over to Aunt Peg's house and play Hearts with her, her husband Uncle Bill and their son Tim. When I was in town, I was invited to join the game. Aunt Peg's gentle personality came through in her card playing. I probably took advantage of her niceness. Since they played for money, Gram covered my losses and because she spoiled me, I got to keep my winnings.

The most traumatic death while I was in college though was the assassination of President Kennedy.

It was a Friday afternoon and between classes someone said something about the President being shot. This seemed so weird that everyone thought it was just a rumor. There was no reason to believe it. This was long before 24-hour news and there was no way to confirm or deny the rumor so everyone headed off to their next class. My next class was chemistry lab. Near the beginning of the class, I had to get some material for an experiment from the lab storeroom. The men working in the storeroom had their radio on. This was strange as they should not have had the radio on during class. So I listened to what was being said. Someone on the radio was saying that a foreign leader, whose name I didn't recognize, extended his condolences to the American people in their time of great tragedy. Remembering the rumors before class started, I realized that the report of President Kennedy being shot wasn't a rumor, it was true. It felt like a kick in the gut. I went back and interrupted the class, which suddenly seemed very unimportant. We listened to the radio in silence until we were told that all classes for the day were canceled and everyone should go home. I joined the mass of students walking away from the academic buildings. Some people were crying. I was too stunned to cry. There was also fear. Initially no one knew who the assassin was. It hadn't been that long ago that we had gathered in the dorm's dining room to listen to Kennedy's report to the nation on the Cuban Missile Crisis. Were the Russians behind his death?

When I got to the dorm, the TV was on. It would stay on most of the time until TV coverage ended on Monday after the funeral. I spent some time watching the proceedings and the TV room was always full. I missed the moment when Oswald was killed at the police station as I was out walking. I spent a lot of time walking that weekend. It was a good way for me to deal with strong emotions. Wearing myself out physically didn't leave any energy to use on emotions. I was stunned that something like this could happen in the United States. We were a civilized country. People didn't get shot and killed. I hadn't been a big Kennedy fan but he was my President, and it was doubly sad to see a young, vibrant man cut down so early. And it was so sad to see his family. The salute from three-year-old John-John as his father's casket went by was so poignant.

Since I was so far away from the family, who were still in Hawaii, I wrote them a long letter, sharing my feelings of a world gone crazy. I took all weekend to write the letter. Mail wouldn't be picked up for delivery until Monday so I had time.

***

The student unrest that was to impact so many colleges and universities during the late 1960s hadn't reached Marquette by the time I graduated. But I was aware of the two biggest drivers of that unrest, the civil rights movement and Vietnam.

In my house, Martin Luther King was viewed as a troublemaker. And the actions of the white college students who went to Mississippi to register black voters were also considered to be the actions of troublemakers. Dad categorized people into those who followed traditional rules and those who didn't. I was still accepting of his view of the world. His views at the time were mainstream views. And with Marquette being a mainstream Catholic university, I wasn't exposed to many divergent views.

We were for Goldwater in 1964. His support of the military and his willingness to praise the actions of the advisors we had sent to Vietnam resonated well with my parents. The head navy man in Vietnam was a classmate of Dad's from the Naval Academy. Captain S. could only be doing good things.

**

Just because I started college in a premed program didn't mean that I graduated from college ready to go to medical school. Halfway through my fourth semester of chemistry I decided that if I never took another chemistry class it would be too soon. Of course four semesters of chemistry was nothing as a minor required five semesters, so I took the fifth semester and added a minor in chemistry to my major in mathematics.

My lack of interest in chemistry wasn't the only reason I dropped out of premed. The counselors at Marquette frequently talked about how difficult it was for a woman to make it through medical school. It was a variant on the "girls don't" theme. After all, a man in medical school would probably be married and his wife could support him. A woman in medical school, even if she was married, couldn't expect to have her husband support her. A man supporting his wife's career was a foreign concept in the 1960s. And there was a third reason. I was beginning to wonder if medicine was the right field for me. It clearly would provide the mental stimulation that I craved. But it required too much interaction with other people. I was discovering that I was happiest when I was alone and working on a difficult problem.

Deciding not to follow a medical career left me in a quandary about what to do next. I didn't know that there was a job called mathematician that I could have considered. And none of my math teachers or career counselors told me about it. The most common suggestion was that I could teach mathematics.

The nudge toward my next career idea came from Tom, the fellow student I was dating early in my junior year. I'd met him in a history class. He also shared my interest in mathematics. He was quiet and studious and had an interest in music that went far beyond the pop music that I was interested in. One of his favorite composers was Bartok. Tom was the first "townie" I'd dated and since he and his mother lived close to campus, I was periodically invited over for dinner. I enjoyed the break from dorm food.

I discovered that Tom could be found hanging out in the university's computer area. My introduction to computers was "keypunching" his programs. In those days, programs and most data were entered into a computer using punched cards. These stiff, heavy paper cards were standardized at $3\frac{1}{4}$ by $7\frac{3}{8}$ inches. They were eighty columns wide and twelve rows high. A keypunch machine was used to punch the computer coding for letters, numbers and special characters onto these cards using a standard QWERTY keyboard. To facilitate keypunching, programs were hand coded onto to coding sheets which contained eighty boxes per line corresponding to the eighty columns on a punched card.

Tom and I stopped dating the spring of 1965. I liked him but couldn't see myself married to him.

By then I was hooked on computers. I learned to program by taking both of the computer classes that Marquette offered. Only one was for credit. I never saw the university's computer as students were not allowed into the computer room. We submitted the deck of punched cards containing our programs into cubbyholes next to the computer room. Our punched cards and printed output were returned to us in the same area after the job was run. I learned the computer language FORTRAN in the not-for-credit class. It was the language used by engineers and scientists to solve mathematical problems. In the for-credit Introduction to Computer Programming class we used the Assembly Language for the IBM 7074, the university's computer, to code programs. The class was designed to get us as close to the computer's actual machine code as possible. We started with a handful of commands. They included such basic commands as: ADD, MOVE, GOTO and IF. Using those basic commands we had to create the functionality of more advanced commands before we could use them. The assignment to code the MULTIPLY command was challenging. One of our projects was to write a bootstrap loader. I had two years of programming experience before I realized how impressive this accomplishment was. This was my favorite class of my entire college career.

One other advantage of dropping out of premed was that after graduation I could stop going to school. Some of my classmates were going on to graduate school, but I was ready to become a productive member of society. There were jobs available in the new field of computer programming and I went looking for one.

I accepted a job at the Federal Deposit Insurance Corporation (FDIC) in Washington, D. C. In the months before I graduated, I'd interviewed for a number of computer programmer jobs. I vividly remember the opening comment from one hiring manager.

"We don't usually hire girls as they just get pregnant and leave."

The FDIC job was the best of all the jobs I'd looked at. I was interviewed for that job because a friend of my parents, Mrs. R, whose son Curtis had been in my third and fourth grade classes, had gotten back in touch with Mom and Dad after they returned to Virginia. Mrs. R knew the manager at FDIC whose department was being expanded to include a computer. They were hiring to staff a new group that would be responsible for that computer. No one knew much about what made a good computer programmer, and I didn't do anything silly during the interview so they hired me. I was scheduled to start working at FDIC at the end of June to give me some vacation time after graduation.

***

On the love and marriage front, I'd been told that men weren't attracted to smart women and that I had to defer to boys and let them be the smart ones. I couldn't do it. Then I met David and finally found someone who appreciated me because I was smart. And the physical attraction had been there from the beginning. He wasn't someone who would stand out in a crowd. He was medium height and medium weight with light brown hair and brown eyes. But I thought he was cute.

We met early my senior year. David was living in the first floor apartment in the same apartment building where my roommate Joanne and I were living in the third floor apartment. Joanne had actually met David before I did and invited him over to our apartment to watch TV. On our first date he recounted that evening.

"I saw these interesting eyes watching me and I knew I had to get to know you better."

He had graduated the year before and was working in Milwaukee as a salesman. He was the first person to give me flowers, a bouquet of salmon colored gladiolas. They are still my favorite flower.

Our relationship developed slowly but David and I got "pinned" shortly before I graduated from college. I always knew he was smart, but when he gave me his fraternity pin to wear I wasn't expecting it to be a Phi Beta Kappa pin. The main thing that kept us from talking seriously about marriage was that David was leaving to join the army. With the Vietnam War going on, he decided he would get an officer's commission instead being drafted. Things were serious enough between us that I was to keep his car at my house, actually my parents' house, until he returned from his initial army training. All the things that I had acquired during my college career got moved to Virginia in David's car. We drove together on that trip. My parents did not object to our traveling together as the trip could be made in a single day.

Unlike my Dad, David had no interest in making the military his career. He grew up in Oregon where his family still lived. His plan was to move back there after he got out of the army. And, of course, I would go with him. I was looking forward to having some permanence in my life, to live in one place for a long time. Just because I coped with the disruption of Dad's frequent moves didn't mean I enjoyed that.

He met my parents when they came to Milwaukee for my graduation. The initial meeting, a lunch to celebrate my graduation, went well. There were seven of us at that lunch, David and me, my parents, Uncle Carl and Aunt Regi and Gram. We had gone to Maders, one of the finest restaurants in Milwaukee. It had been too pricy for me to ever visit on a college student's budget, but Dad was paying and wanted to go somewhere special. The memorable thing about the lunch was not that my family and David met for the first time. It was the wine. There was a special on the menu that day, May Wine. So Dad ordered a bottle. It quickly became apparent that the wine was too sweet and too thin so a different wine was ordered.

However, at the end of the meal, the May Wine was gone, and both my mother and aunt, neither of whom ever drank, were slightly tipsy. Everyone got a good laugh out of that.

David gave me my twenty-second birthday present early as he had to leave for army training before the actual date. How could you not love a guy who gave you both a bottle of perfume and a book of puzzles?

Before we left Milwaukee to start our professional lives, Joanne and I made plans to stay in touch. We were both going to be living in Virginia as she was returning to Richmond, the city she grew up in. My parents liked the idea of my living at home and paying them a small amount of rent so I could build up a little nest egg. Lots of people, including my Dad, lived in Virginia and worked in Washington, D.C.

Building a Life

Federal Deposit
Insurance Corporation
(FDIC)

F DIC'S FIRST COMPUTER, an IBM S/360, was installed in
late May 1966. I started working at FDIC as a computer programmer a month later. And for the first time since I'd
lived with Mackie and Gram, it made absolutely no difference
that I had been born a girl.

There were eight or nine novice programmers who
started work that summer and fall at FDIC. Four of us were
women. The logic seemed to be that there was a shortage
of experienced programmers so let's hire people who have
some interest in the field and have some training and see
who works out. As the organization had just come into existence, no one had been in FDIC's computer department

for any length of time. Everyone was as new as I was. Even most of the experienced programmers were young, mostly in their twenties and thirties.

Just like in college, the computer was in a separate air-conditioned room. But unlike in college all programmers had access to the computer room. There were still areas to drop off programs and data and retrieve the output after the computer operator had run your job. By today's standards the computer was very large. The central processing unit (CPU) stood as high as a person and was about three feet wide and two feet deep. On the other hand, by today's standards, it was also very small. Our first machine only had 128 KB of memory. A computer today with 2 GB of memory has over 15,000 times as much memory.

I didn't quite start work at FDIC ready to program. I had learned two programming languages in college, FORTRAN and the Assembly Language for the college's computer, an IBM 7074. Unfortunately FDIC was using COBOL which I didn't know so they handed me a book. It wasn't titled *Read This and Learn COBOL* but that was its purpose. At the end of my fourth day at work, I'd finished the book and was assigned a program to write. Several days later I had completed writing and testing my first "professional" computer program. It was much easier than anything I'd done in college. The difficulty of the programs I was assigned rapidly increased, and I was on my way to being a respected and valued member of the department.

It turned out that I was very good at this thing called computer programming. And I was thoroughly enjoying the work. The challenge of figuring out the logic to make programs work was the mental stimulation I'd been searching for all of my life. I would have done this work for free, and the plus was that they paid me a lot of money to do it.

While I was having a great time in my new job, David was not enjoying his initial army training. But he'd figured out a way to make his life better and showed up on his next visit with a ring and a formal marriage proposal. I was caught off guard as he'd given me no indication of his plan.

"But I can't get married; I'm having too much fun working." I blurted out.

I wasn't the only one caught off guard. David flung the ring, still in its black box, across the room and stormed out. I did manage to patch things up enough that he took the ring with him when he left and perhaps had an understanding that "not now" was not the same as "never." After all David still had almost three years left on his army obligation and quitting my job after only a few months would not be good for my fledgling career. Still, it would be a while before we saw each other again. While I wasn't happy about the rift in our relationship, there was no doubt in my mind that I had my priorities right.

***

Most of the programs the FDIC programmers wrote were to produce reports. One of the more interesting programs I wrote was to produce a directory of all the FDIC insured banks in the United States. The thing that made this interesting was that the data file to be used to create the book was all in upper case letters. And the book, which had been done by typesetting in the past, needed to have both upper and lower case letters. The printer attached to our computer could print both upper and lower cases so my program had to convert the upper case letters to lower case when it was appropriate to do so. For example, the input file contained the characters "BANK." For the most part, that had to be changed to the characters "Bank." The logic needed to do this was tricky in COBOL. So I learned a new computer language, the Assembly Language for the IBM S/360, and wrote a program to produce the book. Determining what the case of a letter should be was a lot harder than it appeared to be at the beginning of the task.

There was a lot of repetitive code in the programs that produced reports. For example, every program had to keep track of how many pages it had printed so that it could put a page number at the bottom of every page and a header at the top of every new page. Each programmer had to add this code to every program they wrote.

Some senior people in the department developed an approach that would speed up the work we were doing. We could develop a new language for programmers to specify the unique aspects of each report. We would then write a program that interpreted this new language, added common report processing and produced the code that actually printed the report.

Since I was now an experienced Assembly Language programmer, I became part of the team assigned to write our new report program generator. One day while I was picking up my computer output, one of the computer operators stopped me.

"You are really having problems with that program aren't you?" he asked.

"No, it's going very well, why do you think I'm having problems?" I was mystified.

"Well," said the operator, "it always blows up."

A program "blowing up" was the term we used to describe a program that ended with a problem. To help a programmer determine the cause of the problem, the system printed out the contents of the computer's memory. You could tell that a program blew up because of the sound that the printer made. In those days, printers were line printers and you could hear them as they printed out a line of data. There was a different sound made when the closely packed data of the computer's memory was printed vs. the sound made when the more space-filled data of a report was printed. The computer operator knew my program always blew up from the sound the printer made. I took pride in explaining that the output from my program was computer code, and I needed to look at what was in the computer's memory at the end of a test in order to check my work. The only way to get a printout of memory was to "blow up" the program.

I'm showing Dad and Chris my program on punched cards in my FDIC office

After the team completed the report program generator, programmers in the department started using it and making suggestions for improvement. There were also complaints about its limitations. I remember John W, the supervisor of the programmers using the new report generator, saying there was no way to do something he needed done. I knew John well as he had been my first boss when I started at FDIC. After staring at the problem for a few minutes I told him how to do what he wanted to do.

I was feeling pleased with my ingenuity and was not prepared for John's irritated response.

"It doesn't matter that a programmer of your caliber can figure out how to do it, I need a less skilled programmer to be able to figure out how to do it." he said.

It was a useful lesson to learn early in my career about developing computer tools for people who were less technically savvy.

***

One of the advantages of my job was that I was making lots of money. Even though I was living at home, I could have afforded a decent apartment. Poor Joanne, who had gotten a job as a social worker, was living in a one-room apartment with a makeshift kitchen because that was all she could afford. But by living at home I could save money for a car and the trip to Europe that Joanne and I started planning before we graduated from college. The other thing I could afford was flying lessons.

I learned to fly at a small airport near Leesburg, Virginia. Since I didn't have a car of my own, I borrowed the family Volkswagen for the forty-minute drive to the airport. Dad made it clear that I was expected to put gas in the car after each trip.

I had my first lesson in September 1966 in a J3, also known as a Piper Cub. It was a "tail dragger," with its third wheel in the back. On my second lesson I was moved to a plane with the newer landing gear, tricycle gear, with the third wheel in the front. It was much easier to land. On my third lesson, I got a new instructor, Dave, who was to shepherd me all the way to my private pilot's license.

Almost from the beginning the student pilot flies the plane during take offs and landings. However, the instructor is always there in case the student does something dangerous. One day, after a landing, when I had about twelve hours of flying time, there was something different.

"Pull off the runway." Dave said. And when I'd done that there was one more instruction.

"Take it around yourself." He opened the door and climbed out.

I was on my own. I took a deep breath and told myself that Dave wouldn't send me up if I couldn't get the plane down. I hesitated slightly at the start of the runway before pushing the throttle forward to accelerate the plane to take-off speed. Once the plane was moving fast enough, I pulled the wheel back and the plane leapt into the air. There was no turning back now. I knew the standard pattern to fly, turn left after I was at pattern altitude, turn left again and fly downwind parallel to the runway, and make a final left turn to head directly for the runway. As I lined the plane up for my first solo landing, I remembered Dave telling me that the biggest problem with landings was trying to do too much. "After all," he said, "these planes are built to land themselves."

My first solo landing was the best landing of my life. I took Dave's advice and just slowed the plane down to landing speed and let the plane land by itself.

Mary the pilot

With my solo flight out of the way, I could take the plane up by myself and promptly demonstrated how stupid student pilots could be. We'd had a stretch of bad weather that kept me from flying and one day when the weather was marginal, I decided I needed to fly. Dave wasn't at the airport that day so I browbeat the youngest instructor, who was actually younger than I was, into signing off on my taking a plane up. Dave would have never let me go up as spring storms in Virginia are nothing to fool with, a fact I quickly learned once the plane was in the air. The turbulent weather with thunder and lightning around is much scarier in the air than on the ground. The black sky in the direction of the storm was much more ominous at eye level than it was looking up at it. And, with the speed of the airplane, distance provided less protection from the storm. When one is standing still a person feels quite far away from a lightning strike only a few miles distant. But when you are flying at over a hundred miles an hour, you can cover those few miles quickly. Fortunately, I was able to get down safely and learned a valuable lesson.

We then moved on to challenging things like stalls, where you deliberately make the plane stop flying and have to recover as it is dropping out of the sky. A plane needs speed to fly and if you slow the plane's speed enough, it stops flying. Stalls are easy to recover from. You just add speed and the plane starts flying again. We practiced stalls frequently but I never lost the sinking feeling in the pit of my stomach when the plane stopped flying. Still, my response to the problem became instinctive, which was the whole purpose of the exercise.

I learned the basics of instrument flying. I had to wear a hood that kept me from looking out the window, and I had to rely on the instrument panel to see what the plane was doing. After I had practiced flying using just instruments, Dave would take control of the plane, tell me to look at my lap and spin the plane around a bit. At some point he would say "it's yours," and it was never flying straight and level when I got it back. My job was to use the instruments to make it fly straight and level.

The lesson I hated most was called "turns around a point." The objective was to pick a point on the ground, a tree in field worked well, and fly in a circle keeping the plane wing always pointed at the tree. The thing that makes this maneuver tricky is that the wind is always changing direction relative to the plane as you make the circle and you have to compensate for the wind direction changes. I wondered why I was paying good money for this torture.

Just because I could land a plane at my home airport didn't mean my training in how to land a plane stopped. I learned to navigate in the air by flying to other airports. Since most small airports in those days had no radio communication with planes, I got radio practice by flying into Baltimore International Airport. Unlike a landing at a small airport, there was no standard pattern to fly. The tower kept giving me instructions and when they said "you are cleared to land" there was a runway directly in front of me. Another memorable landing was at a small airport near the ocean. It had a short, narrow runway and on the day we went there, we weren't landing into the wind, we had a crosswind. The wind was coming at the plane from the side. I made a comment about how small the runway was. Dave, as usual, was encouraging.

"There is plenty of room to land. You just need to put the plane down near the start of the runway."

With the short runway and the crosswind it was a tricky landing and it was comforting to have Dave sitting next to me in case I got in trouble. After I made a successful landing, Dave congratulated me and then he reminded me that picking my landing spot was something I should do on all landings, not just on short runways.

In addition to flying lessons, I took flight school classes at the local junior college at night. Passing a written exam was a required step on my way to a pilot's license. After doing a solo flight to another airport, I knew it was only a matter of time before Dave told me to schedule my flight test.

The flight test was at an airport that I'd never been to and it was a solo flight there and back. I don't remember much about the test but it seemed easier than many of my lessons. I was so excited on my flight home that I felt the plane was bouncing up and down as I flew. The flight examiner had called Leesburg to let them know I'd passed, and Dave was not the only one lined up to congratulate me. Every other pilot on the ground that day offered me their congratulations.

My first passenger as a licensed pilot was Gram. She had moved in with the family when we moved back to Virginia in 1964. Sometimes she drove with me to Leesburg and was waiting for me when I finished my lesson. I think, at least once, Dave allowed her to fly in the back seat during a lesson. She hadn't gone with me the day I passed my flight test as I was gone for hours that day.

***

I didn't have much time to use my newly earned private pilot's license as several months later on November 1, 1967, Joanne and I headed off on our long planned three month trip to Europe. We had a vague itinerary. The only firm dates were the day we were scheduled to pick up my new Volkswagen Beetle at the Volkswagen factory and three dates for mail pickup in specific cities. In the days before electronic messaging letters were the primary way to keep in touch. American Express offices in Europe served as drop boxes where people could send letters to travelers. These would be held until the addressee picked them up.

My initial plan had been to quit my job and go to Europe. But my ever-practical Dad had a suggestion.

"Ask them for a leave of absence. If you take a leave of absence, your medical insurance will remain in effect."

FDIC was happy to give me a leave of absence.

Armed with our copy of *Europe on $5 a Day*, Joanne and I boarded a train in Washington, D.C., and headed for New York City. Gram, Mom, Dan and Chris came to see us off. We flew Icelandic Airlines to Europe because it had the cheapest flights available. Even though most planes going to Europe were jets by then, Icelandic still flew propeller planes. This necessitated a stop en route. We arrived in Reykjavik, Iceland, in the middle of the night. They wouldn't let us out of the airport but I still added Iceland as the fourth country I'd been in. The United States, Canada and Japan were the first three. By the time we returned home three months later, my count of countries visited was up to eleven.

Joanne and me leaving for Europe

On My Own

I CAME BACK from Europe and had to start thinking about the future. It was only a matter of time before Dad got orders again. This time I didn't have to uproot my life and move with the family. David and I had stayed in touch after I turned down his marriage proposal, but over time, letters became further and further apart. I hadn't heard from him since before I went to Europe so I only had myself to consider in my plans for the future. The people at FDIC were glad to have me back, and I was glad to be back at work. While I was in Europe, a new college graduate, Sarah, had joined the computer department at FDIC. Sarah had been living at her parents' home in Annapolis, Maryland, and was looking for an apartment. She was also looking for a roommate, and I agreed that having a roommate was a better choice at this stage of my life than having a place on my own. So we found an apartment in Washington, D.C., within walking distance of the office.

In spite of being in Washington, D.C., or maybe because I was in Washington, D.C., the turmoil in the country in 1968 seemed far away. But one April evening the turmoil intruded on my life. Joanne and I had been on a driving trip. We arrived back in the D.C. area and saw large amounts of smoke rising over the city. Rather than going into D.C. to my apartment, our planned destination, we headed to my parents' house. We found out there that Martin Luther King Jr. had been assassinated. It is disappointing that the importance of what King was doing had not yet become apparent to me; the only actual memory I have of the event is the personal inconvenience it caused.

I don't remember any violence in D.C. after Robert Kennedy was assassinated less than two months later, but I do remember the sadness of the train trip that brought his body back to Washington, D.C.. And the huge crowds along the train route.

That summer Dad got his orders and the family moved back to Bremerton. This was to be Dad's last tour of duty before retiring and the navy allowed him to select his duty station. Mom and Dad had really enjoyed living in Bremerton. The plan was that Dad's last years on active duty in the U.S. Navy would be where they would live after retirement. Since I had a good job and a shared apartment, there was no reason for me to move with the family. I stayed in D.C.

In addition to being a good roommate, Sarah opened my eyes to the world of clothes. She knew a small shop where the owner had this wonderful collection of clothes for young women. I had never spent much money on clothes so this was a new experience. My first purchase was a winter coat. I tried on many coats that just weren't me. Then the shop owner brought me a medium blue double-breasted, tailored coat with large pockets.

"Try this one," she said.

It was perfect. She understood that I wasn't a frilly person and had sorted out what I liked in clothes. I quickly went from being a skeptic about the clothes in her shop to a true believer. Over the next six months or so, I acquired a wonderful wardrobe. I still remember the pink shirt-style dress with a gold paisley pattern on it, and the black and white patterned suit with a box jacket and a flared skirt. Both pieces of the suit were trimmed in black faux leather.

My career was progressing as well. Unbeknownst to me, I was developing a reputation as a programmer beyond our department. I learned of my growing reputation when I got a call from a recruiter with a lead on a non-government job. I went to the interview but the job didn't seem to offer more than what I had. It was for more money than I was making at the moment, but I was only a couple of months away from a raise at FDIC. I ended up turning down the job but it was nice to be wanted.

In the months after the family moved to Bremerton, I became aware of how few ties I had to the Washington, D.C.

area. There was a moment of surprise when I realized that I had to make plans for Thanksgiving. I couldn't just show up at home. There were after-work outings with people from the office, but I wasn't meeting new people, and many of my colleagues were married with families and lives of their own. I wasn't piloting a plane as often as I had expected to because I didn't have people to fly with me. Going flying by myself was fine, but it got old without someone to share it with. None of the people I worked with had any interest in flying and I had no idea about how to become part of the flying community at the airport. That October, when Sarah met the man of her dreams and made plans to get married, I realized I didn't know anyone to replace her as a roommate.

And there was this tiny fly in the ointment at work. I loved being a programmer, but they wanted to make me a programming supervisor. I turned down the first offer of a promotion to supervisor in mid-1968. I was having an unusual problem for a woman at the time. Most women my age tell stories of being bypassed for promotions, especially in the 1960s and 1970s. These promotions went instead to men with less experience. I was benefiting from the newness of the business computer field and the philosophy that said you should promote your best technical staff to supervisory positions. There was an older woman in the office, Pat, in her mid-30s, who would have been a much better choice for programming supervisor than I was. She was a reasonably good programmer, was mature and had better people skills than I did. But because she wasn't a great programmer and maybe because she was a woman, no one thought about promoting her. Neither bypassing women for promotion or exclusively promoting the best technicians made a lot of sense, but that was the way things were done.

In late December 1968, I took a flight to Bremerton to celebrate Christmas with the family. While I was there I made a side trip to visit my cousin Paul's family in Yakima, Washington, on the eastern side of the Cascade Mountains. I spent the night with them and when I woke up the next morning it was snowing hard. My flight home had been cancelled. Since I had a date for the New Year's Eve party that night, I decided to take the train home. Unfortunately, the snow continued and I spent New Year's Eve on a train stuck in a tunnel through the Cascades. My parents had been monitoring the train's progress as they were going to pick me up when I arrived. They let my date for that evening know I wasn't going to make the party.

One of the important things that happened while I was in Bremerton was that *Apollo 8* circled the moon. The first earthrise picture was transmitted back to Earth and the crew read Genesis. I've seen replays of this many times since then and I have memories of the *Apollo 11* landing on the moon, but I have no actual memories of *Apollo 8*. This is surprising to me given my interest in space and going to the moon.

Since I was on the west coast I added a visit to San Francisco to see some friends before returning to D.C. I wasn't really thinking about moving when I made my plane reservations to visit San Francisco after Bremerton, but the seeds of the move had certainly been planted by my dissatisfaction with my life in D.C. I felt more comfortable in San Francisco the few days I was there than I did when I returned to my D.C. apartment where I'd lived for almost a year.

San Francisco felt like home which in some ways seemed rather strange. Even though I was born in the San Francisco Bay Area, went to kindergarten there and spent two years of high school actually in San Francisco, the total time I lived in that area was only about three years. I had lived in both Bremerton and the Washington, D.C. area longer than that. It may have been because we lived in San Francisco during my high school years and I was able to explore the city on my own. As a result, I had gotten to know it better than other places we had lived. Or it might have been the weather. I was treated to typical January weather in California—lots of blue sky and temperatures in the low 60s. When I returned to Washington, D.C. it was a typical January day there. The temperature might have made it into the 40s. The skies were gray and there was dirty snow on the ground.

The day I returned to work, I had an announcement for my boss.

"I'm giving you a month's notice; I'm moving to San Francisco." I said.

The fact that I didn't have a job in San Francisco wasn't an issue as far as I was concerned. I was sure that I could easily find another. The two and a half years at FDIC had given my career a great start. I wasn't the only one who thought that California was a better place to live than the east coast.

My boss had lived in the San Francisco Bay Area and clearly wasn't surprised by my decision.

"I expected you to walk into my office first thing this morning and tell me that. Why did you wait until the afternoon?" he asked.

I gave a month's notice when I quit FDIC to give me time to either finish up things I was working on or properly turn them over to someone else. It also gave me time to close down the apartment and get rid of all the furniture in it. With Sarah getting married she had planned to move out soon anyway. I packed my belongings into a few shippable boxes and sent them to Mr. and Mrs. C who had been our across-the-street neighbors when we had lived in San Francisco while I was in high school. Mom had kept in touch with Mrs. C and was slightly more comfortable with my move with the knowledge that there was an old friend of hers around. The only piece of furniture I kept was a carved wooden chair that had belonged to Gram. I gave it to Joanne for safekeeping but somehow never got it back.

Then David called one Saturday morning. He was stationed in Panama and had just finished a business trip in Washington, D.C. He only had the afternoon free before his plane left for home but that was enough time for him to come over to my apartment for a visit. It had been over a year since we had had any contact but we were instantly comfortable being together again. We talked about my trip to Europe and his living in Panama. He was interested in what I was doing with my pilot's license. Then he brought up the subject of my job. It was, after all, a touchy subject as I'd chosen the job over him.

"Oh, I've quit my job; I'm in the process of moving to San Francisco."

"What are you going to do in San Francisco?" I could hear concern in his voice.

"I'll find another job. I shouldn't have any problem doing that. There's just nothing to keep me in Washington, D.C."

The furrow that had begun to appear on his brow disappeared and he smiled. "For a moment there, I thought maybe you were moving to get married."

"No, nothing like that," I smiled back. "San Francisco seems like a nicer place to live than Washington, D.C." I hadn't burned all of my bridges when I chose my job over David two years earlier.

"How are you getting to San Francisco?" He asked after a pause. My description of driving around Europe had given him the impression that I was willing to drive across the country.

"I'm flying."

"Panama is between Washington, D.C. and San Francisco." he said after another pause.

So I made my plane reservations to fly to San Francisco by way of Panama.

***

My last task before leaving Washington, D.C. was to sell the Volkswagen Beetle that had carried us around Europe. It had been a good and trusty car but I wasn't driving across the country. Selling it and getting a new car in San Francisco made sense. The move to San Francisco was a major milestone in my life. For the first time I was the one to decide where I was going to live.

The first stop on the flight to my new life was in Miami. I never left the airport but I was on the ground and so I added Florida as my forty-sixth state visited.

David met me at the airport in Panama. He was driving a yellow MGB3. A big step up from the boxy dark gray Dodge Dart he had been driving when I graduated from college.

He had an off-base apartment where we stayed during my visit. I demonstrated my cooking skills in his kitchen but my first dinner made us sick. Stomach problems. The doctor thought perhaps I hadn't washed the produce carefully enough. It was one of the things you had to be aware of not being in a first-world country. The tourist areas were safe for eating and drinking but once when we were wandering in a poor area of Panama City, and I wanted a Coke, David took me to a fancy hotel for my drink.

We didn't get to see much of the canal. It was hard to get close and we didn't have time for a trip through it. David thought we could use my pilot's license and see it from the air, but it turned out my United States pilot's license wasn't good in Panama and I felt too rusty to take a flight test and get a Panama pilot's license.

Before I'd left for San Francisco, David reminded me he was getting out of the army in September. "And," he said, "we could get married then."

"Sounds like a plan to me," I replied.

San Francisco - 1969

I ARRIVED IN San Francisco in early February 1969. My first priority was finding a place to live. Rental prices were higher than they had been in D.C. and I quickly decided I needed to look at studio apartments, not one-bedroom apartments. I found a furnished studio on Sacramento Street just off of Van Ness Avenue for a price I thought I could afford. It didn't have access to the backyard of the converted Victorian, but it did have a view of the yard. I retrieved all of my worldly possessions that I'd shipped west to our old neighbors. Mrs. C looked at my meager household possessions and gave me a few more items, mostly linens. And I moved into my new home.

Then I went looking for a job. My search of the *San Francisco Chronicle* help wanted section provided several leads. I was expecting to be able to make more money than I had been making at FDIC, but the first two jobs I interviewed for offered less money. I had a reference from Bob, one of the programmers I had worked with at FDIC. Bob was a retired army warrant officer and one of his friends, also a warrant officer, was still on active duty, working with computers for the Sixth Army in San Francisco. So I called Bob's friend, Wally, and set up an appointment to talk to him. After a brief chat, Wally took me into see the Colonel. The Colonel was happy to answer any questions I had but made it clear that since Wally's friend Bob had recommended me so strongly, he was willing to offer me a job on the spot at my old salary.

"Bob says you are great and we should hire you immediately." Wally reassured me when I expressed doubt at the quickness of the offer.

So I accepted one of the open positions that they had. Just like at FDIC, I would be developing tools for other programmers to use and troubleshooting difficult problems.

The environment at the Sixth Army was different than the environment at FDIC. The difference wasn't because it was military. Actually the staff was mostly civilian. The difference was that everyone was older. Bob, whose recommendation had gotten me the job, was over forty and was old by FDIC standards. His friend Wally, who was probably a few years younger than Bob, was about the age of most of the staff. It would not have been a good first job for me, but I had serious experience by then. Government Service (GS) jobs had numeric levels, the higher the level the more senior the job. As a GS-11, the level I'd reached at FDIC, I was coming in as a senior person. I was accepted quickly as a good addition to the staff, and I continued to enjoy what I was doing.

My original plan had been to delay getting a new car as San Francisco still had the great public transit system I'd remembered from high school. But when I started working in the Presidio, where the Sixth Army was headquartered, there was no public transportation going onto the army base. So I had to buy a car. I considered buying another Volkswagen Beetle, but was intrigued by the new Japanese cars made by a company called Toyota. The Corolla was about the same price as a Beetle and seemed more finished. I got a light blue one.

David and I began another stretch of a long-distance relationship. But unlike 1966, we both had phones and scheduled regular phone calls. The fact that David was in a foreign country did make it more expensive to keep in touch but we both were making reasonable money. This time my relationship with David was more of a priority for me. I was ready to get married. More and more of the people around me were married. And I was no longer worried about my career. I knew that I had experience in a growing field and would be able to get a job anywhere. And for the first time I had contact with David's family. His mother started the conversation by writing me a long, newsy letter welcoming me to the family.

Everything was going fine. And then I met Tony.

Tony was one of the analysts working in the office. The first time we ever talked was at an office bowling league match. For years he told the story that we met when he dropped his bowling ball on my foot. He hadn't. But it made a good story and let his sense of humor shine through.

The bowling league was a way to get to know people in the office better. I was an awful bowler and wasn't a useful addition to any of the teams. I substituted if someone was missing from a team and I made myself useful by keeping score. Then Tony invited me to join his team and started coaching me on how to bowl better. When he asked me out for dinner after work, I suspected that he might be interested in me as more than just a co-worker. When I hesitated, he was nonchalant.

"It's just dinner. No big deal if you don't want to join me."

Tony was older. He was forty when I met him. His boyish good looks were long gone by then but his compact muscular build still showed the athlete he had been. When he told me he had gone to college on a football scholarship, I wasn't surprised. His hairline was receding but he didn't look old. And he certainly didn't act old. Usually lively guys found me dull so Tony's attention was something new. I found him very attractive. And I went out to dinner with him.

Years later my brother Chris said to me, "I know why you married Tony. He walked with a swagger."

Sometimes, after bowling, part of the group would go to the Presidio Officers' Club for a drink. It was on one of those evenings that I found out that Tony was divorced and had three children. The youngest was already a teenager. The children either lived with their mother or were on their own. Somewhere in that conversation Tony mentioned that he wanted to get married again but had no interest in having any more children.

After that conversation with Tony, I found myself thinking about new possibilities. I had never considered the idea that I could get married and not have children. While I was getting comfortable with the idea of being married, having children still bothered me. I could just see me turning into my mother. In spite of my attitude of doing my own thing, even if it was something that "girls didn't do," a part of me always longed to be "normal." And this meant marrying David and having a family with him like my parents had. Up until then, I hadn't thought of Tony as a possible husband. The new path I now saw before me meant rejecting my view of a normal life and considering a new way of life. But I so much didn't want to turn into my mother. She was a smart, capable woman whose life was dedicated to raising children and saying yes to what her husband wanted.

I was now paying the price for always making my own decisions. I had no one to confide in and with whom to discuss my concerns. So I took the step that I thought would buy me time. I broke up with David again. I told him I couldn't deal with this long-distance relationship and that we'd get together after he got out of the army. It was only a few months away at that time.

What I didn't realize was that by taking that approach, I *was* effectively making a decision. Tony had been low key about forming a relationship with me as I was engaged to someone else. But once I broke the engagement, he pressed his suit aggressively. He took pains to assure me that my career was important to him and he wanted me to keep working.

We watched the *Apollo 11* moon landing together at Tony's apartment. He had a TV, I didn't. He seemed as excited about the historic event as I was. Most people remember Neil Armstrong's words as he stepped out of the lunar module onto the surface of the moon: "That's one small step for [a] man, one giant leap for mankind."

But that was hours after the landing. The words that I remember most vividly were right after the lunar module touched down. Armstrong said, "Houston, Tranquility Base here. The Eagle has landed."

I still get choked up when I hear those words. Mackie had been right when he told me that someday people would go to the moon. We had just landed two men safely there.

It was over six hours between the landing and the first step on the moon. I spent part of the time talking about childhood dreams and being so excited that part of them had come true. My going to the moon was the part that hadn't yet come true. Tony was much more grounded about what was going on. He told me he didn't want me to go to the moon while we were married. But to allow me to do what I wanted to do, he would sign an eighty-eight-year contract, not a "until death do us part" contract, and I could go to the moon after the eighty-eight-year contract was up. I was charmed and accepted his proposal.

My parents were not happy when I told them. They insisted I come up to Bremerton and talk about it. I suspect that they might have been able to come up with an argument that I would have listened to but they took the worst possible approach. Tony was a Catholic. A divorced Catholic. So we couldn't be married in the church and thus our marriage would not be valid in the eyes of God. The silly arbitrary rules again. I didn't accept any of it. Tony and I were married in Nevada in early August. In what was to be my last act of financial extravagance for a long time, I flew Joanne out from Virginia to be my maid of honor. One of the couples Tony and I knew from work were camping at Lake Tahoe the weekend we got married. So the husband, Fred, became our best man. A small but nice wedding ceremony.

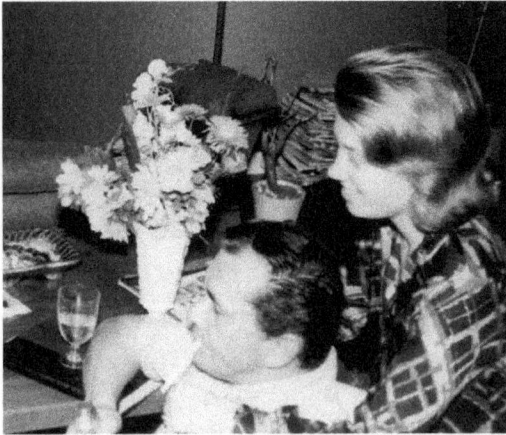

Tony and me

The office threw us a "happy wedding" party when we returned to work. I found out later that there was a rumor floating around that the reason we got married so quickly was that I was pregnant.

There was one important thing I still needed to do. I had to tell David. I wasn't up to calling him directly. I convinced myself that he might not even follow up on the plan from our last discussion of calling me when he got out of the army. Still, when I moved out of my studio apartment into Tony's one-bedroom apartment, I put his, now our, phone number as the forwarding number. David did call. And it was a short conversation as I told him my new status. Tony was upset that I'd forwarded my old number, but I was glad I did.

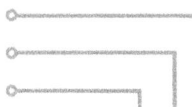

Daly City and Tiburon

W E MADE TONY'S apartment in Daly City, just south of San Francisco, our new home. It was larger than my furnished studio apartment that fortunately had a month-to-month lease.

The apartment complex had a pool but the pool wasn't useful. Either it was fogged in or, if the sun was shining, the wind was also blowing and the pool had "whitecaps" on it. But it had an outside area where we could barbeque or more accurately, Tony could barbeque. He was an excellent cook. I was starting to expand my cooking repertoire and had recently discovered Julia Child. Tony wasn't thrilled with Julia Child so I was happy to leave the cooking to him.

Problems started to emerge with the marriage almost immediately. I discovered that Tony didn't just drink when we were partying, he drank every evening. And then there was the money problem.

When I married Tony I knew he was not in good financial shape. He had been unemployed for a while before getting the job at the Sixth Army. And he had all the debts from his previous marriage to pay off. But I had had no idea how really bad it was. But we had two good incomes and it was possible to pay off his debts. My going into the marriage debt-free helped a lot. The problem was that Tony wanted to keep spending lots of money. He didn't like my new Toyota. And his four-seat Thunderbird was old and needed repair. So his plan was to get rid of both of our cars and buy a new TR-6, a sporty two-seat convertible. The one he chose was dark blue. In spite of my better judgment, I let myself be talked into the plan. I had grown up in a household without much money so I knew how to live on a budget. Tony had grown up with even less money than me but he'd gotten used to spending money. So while I was working on getting rid of his old debts, we were building up new debts, including credit card debts.

One night, about a year after we were married, we had a major argument. We'd argued about the same things before; I didn't like his drinking and spending habits and he didn't like that I wasn't taking better care of my looks. But this time it escalated and I got so mad I stormed out the door and walked until I calmed down. It took me about two hours to achieve that goal. It didn't quite take me two hours to get home as I hadn't walked in a straight line away from the house but it did take quite a while. Not living in San Francisco, there was no public transit to use to get home and since this was before the days of cell phones, I couldn't call and ask to be picked up.

Tony's response when I returned home was surprisingly neutral. There was no indication that he was mad at me for leaving. I did detect a tiny bit of relief on his face but it barely registered as an emotion. Since I had calmed down, I tried to talk about what had happened but Tony wasn't interested.

"You're home. What is there to talk about? It's bedtime; I'm going to bed." His response left me perplexed.

I eventually realized that this was another aspect of Tony's ability to live in the now. It was one of the things about him that originally attracted me. When we were having fun, his ability to enjoy the moment dragged me out of my head and helped me also enjoy the moment. But if we couldn't talk about our problems, how were we ever going to solve them?

It took almost a year and a half but Tony's old debts were finally paid off. The collection agencies stopped calling and we had some financial breathing space, even if we still had our newer debt. The fact that both Tony and I had been promoted one level to GS-12 had helped a lot. Buying a house, which was what Tony wanted to do, was totally out of the question. With no savings we had no money for a down payment. But he came up with another plan. We had been taking trips to the Sierras as we both liked fishing and just being in the outdoors. So Tony suggested we buy land in the Sierras, build a cabin and rent it out when we weren't using it. There was a new area being developed on

Highway 4 near the small town of Dorrington that we could get into for almost no money down. The plan seemed doable. We found property that was zoned for multiple buildings and laid out a plan that included retirement sometime in the future. Our plans had two cabins on the lower part of the property to rent out and a bigger cabin on the upper part of the property for us to retire to. We signed a contract to buy the land and to build the first of the small cabins. It used up all the contingencies in our budget, but it was an investment in the future.

The ink was barely dry on the contract to buy the property in the Sierras before Tony started talking about a new apartment. Admittedly the Daly City apartment was small and basic, but our budget wouldn't support much more. Tony was persistent and late summer 1972 we moved to a townhouse in Tiburon, just north of San Francisco in Marin County. Our new home rented for about twice what we were paying for the apartment in Daly City. It had a pool and the weather in Tiburon was much more suited for using a pool. It was another example of Tony living in the moment, and we were back to running up debt.

But we had good times too. Tony and I had other fun activities besides trips to the Sierras. He had played football in college and remained an active fan. I had watched the Redskins when I lived in Washington, D.C. but quickly became a 49ers fan. The first fall I was in the San Francisco area, the 49ers were still playing at Kezar Stadium near Golden Gate Park. We didn't make all the home games but went to many of them. Then in 1971 the 49ers were scheduled to move to Candlestick Park. Because Candlestick was a bigger stadium than Kezar, the 49ers were selling new season tickets. We got our money in quickly as did Tony's sister Rosemary and her husband, Howard. They lived in Belmont, California, with their six children. Since they were less than twenty miles from our Daly City home, we saw them regularly. We started a new tradition with the 1971 football season. Each home game was preceded by a tailgate party.

The first trip that Tony and I took together was to San Juan Capistrano. Friends of Tony's had come to California and invited us to join them on that part of their trip south. Since we were so close to Mexico we drove across the border to Tijuana and I upped my count of countries visited to thirteen.

We made several trips in 1972. That spring we took a ten-day trip to Hawaii, increasing our credit card debt. Waikiki had changed a lot in the eight years since I had left. And not for the better, lots more concrete buildings and traffic. We did go out and see the house my family had lived in and it hadn't changed. Later that year we went back to Waukegan, Illinois, and drove Tony's parents' household goods out to California. They were getting older and their old neighborhood was deteriorating. Both Tony and Rosemary felt better having them closer. The final trip that year was to southern California to visit with Tony's two daughters and their families. It was the first time Tony had met his three grandchildren. I met Tony's son the following year.

We didn't see much of my family but the third Christmas Tony and I were married we went up to Bremerton for the holidays. Both Dad and Tony were on their best behavior and their initial meeting went well. What I remember most about the visit was Dad being upset about the protestors against the Vietnam War. He told us that he and some other influential citizens in the small town of Bremerton had solved the problem. They had told the editor of the local newspaper that if he didn't stop covering the protests that all advertisers would boycott the newspaper. I was still a supporter of the Vietnam War, but I didn't like the idea of using financial pressure to control newspaper reporting. And it bothered me that Dad thought this was a good idea. Tony wasn't interested in politics and was a supporter of the war so there was no conversation on Dad's announcement. I knew when my opinion didn't matter.

***

After years of defending my right to do all of the things that "girls don't" and mostly winning, I was losing to a more subtle enemy. I felt like I was losing me. I had a real lack of understanding of all the things that made me *me* and tended to not notice the things that I didn't have to fight for while I was growing up. Some of the things I was losing were minor. I'd been playing tennis for a while and enjoyed the outdoor physical activity of the sport. Tony didn't like playing tennis with me. I think it was because I could beat him and being me, I did. The problem was he didn't want me playing tennis with anyone else either.

I wanted to continue being an active pilot. As senior civilian staff of a military organization, we had access to military facilities, including the flying club at Hamilton Air Force Base in northern Marin County. I had made use of the facility as soon as I discovered its existence. Hamilton Air Force Base was pretty far away when we lived in Daly City, and one of the pluses of moving to Marin County for me was that the airport would be closer and I could fly more. But Tony was much happier lounging by the pool than he was going flying. Flying by myself in California got old quickly just as it had when I lived in Washington, D.C.

Spending time in the outdoors had always been important to me. It was one of the reasons for buying property and building a cabin. But lounging by the pool always seemed more important to Tony than using our cabin in the Sierras as a weekend getaway. So I was becoming less active and spending less time outdoors. I hated lounging by the pool.

The age difference between Tony and me didn't seem to be much of a problem, but I wasn't happy that all our friends were older. Tony was the more social of the two of us so he tended to set up activities with other people and most of the people we worked with were closer to his age than mine. I had always picked my friends because they wanted to participate in the intellectual conversations that I enjoyed. There were none of these conversations in my current life. Our friends all seemed pretty set in their ways and not interested in the way the world was changing. Serious conversations about history and science just didn't happen. There were some younger people working in our office. Most of them were young draftees as the Vietnam War was still going on. Some of the draftees were married but social activities with them and their wives almost never happened.

Until late 1972 my career success balanced my marriage frustrations. Initially I was part of a group that produced tools for the other programmers. We also helped troubleshoot difficult programming problems. Then our group began to get smaller. The number of tools we needed to produce for other programmers was shrinking. Big companies, like IBM, were starting to produce and sell the types of digital tools we had been creating. The supervisor of our group was one of the people to leave and I was talked into taking over his job. It wasn't too bad. I had two GIs working for me, Bill and Gordon. They were both good programmers and if they hadn't been draftees and in the army, I would have been working for one of them. Thinking back on the positions we found ourselves in, I think that the positive impact of the Vietnam War on women's rights has been seriously underestimated. It took qualified men out of the running for positions of authority. So women had to be hired and promoted to supervisor. And unlike our World War II mothers, we never gave the jobs back.

I wasn't really interested in the nascent women's liberation movement. I had been so busy trying to forge my own life path that I hadn't noticed that other women were starting to rebel against the "girls don't" culture. Still, when the women in the office asked me to talk to the Colonel about allowing them to wear pant suits to work I was willing to do it. I may have been chosen as the spokesperson because I was the second-most senior woman in the office. Helen, the most senior woman in the office, was the manager of one of the application programming groups. She may have turned them down. Having nice legs, I was perfectly happy to wear dresses to work. So I didn't care about the issue one way or another. But I was successful in getting the Colonel to change the rule. Helen was ten or fifteen years older than I was. I'm sorry I didn't get to know her better and didn't learn her story. Her path to a non-traditional career must have been harder and lonelier than mine had been.

Eventually there was no need for my tool production group. I got transferred into an application area, Demand Analysis, because my troubleshooting skills were needed. We were going to expand the Sixth Army's system to other army computer groups. The initial installation site was Ft. Hood, Texas. And the Demand Analysis portion of the system was chosen as the first part of the system to be installed. I was happy with the transfer to the new group and started making the first of what would become a long string of business trips. Gene, my new boss, was a smart, personable man who had requested that I join his group. I hadn't worked much with Gene as he had had his own computer guru, Dave F. Dave had been a draftee who had stayed with the group for a while after he got out of the army. Before he left the Sixth

Army job to go to Germany, Dave had turned the excellent tool he had produced, "Tapescan," over to me to maintain. I thought I was a good programmer but the level of expertise shown by Dave's work on that utility program was the best I had ever seen. Normally when I was modifying someone else's program, I felt like I had to use the technical equivalent of a hammer or a crowbar to make changes. With changes to Dave's program, I felt like I need to use a scalpel in order to maintain the quality of what he had done.

The process of expanding the Demand Analysis subsystem to the computers at Ft. Hood was educational. Even though they were supposedly running the same computer environment that we were, there turned out to be differences. And nothing worked. For the most part I loved the task of finding out what was wrong. The part I didn't like was the Colonel in charge of the Ft. Hood computer group.

Unlike our Colonel, this army man was convinced that the military tactic of adding more troops to take the hill would work with computer problems. I should have known how to deal with the problem. After all, I'd grown up with a senior military officer who believed strongly in a hierarchy of command. But I was not happy that his meddling slowed down my work. This was especially true when his interference resulted in my out-of-town time being extended. I let my awareness that I was an adult professional and my expectations to be treated like one get in the way of resolving the problem. The Colonel was not happy that I was questioning his judgment. Gene spent more time involved in the Ft. Hood installation than he had planned. He had to smooth out the turmoil I'd created. Eventually we got the system installed. I'd acquired new technical skills during the installation and started to learn the more important lesson of remaining calm when my technical skills were being questioned by senior management.

Shortly after the installation was complete, Gene left to take another job. I was the logical person to take over managing our group. Had there been a man of equal rank in our group, he would have been promoted. However, the rest of the group consisted of a black man, a hippie, a man who was mostly blind, and two enlisted men. Promoting a woman to supervisor, especially one who was a grade higher than anyone else, didn't seem so unusual in light of the other prejudices that existed.

For the first time in my professional career, I was now in the wrong job. One problem was that I knew nothing about Demand Analysis and had no real interest in learning about it. Gene had been the interface between the business office and his technical staff. I had no idea what the business people were talking about when they asked for changes to the system. And they didn't seem to realize that my problem wasn't stupidity, it was just a lack of knowledge. A second problem was that I knew nothing about being a supervisor. And, unlike Gordon and Bill, my new staff included men who had no desire to work for a woman. I did make one decision while I had that job that was to affect the rest of my career. I decided to not even consider that my problems might be that some of the men didn't want to work for a woman. If that were true, then there was nothing I could do about it. I decided my problems had to be that I wasn't a good enough supervisor. That was a problem I thought I could fix.

***

I was now in the unsettling position of having serious problems at work and serious problems at home. And things were getting worse at home. In spite of my resolve to stop having arguments, especially when Tony had been drinking, we kept having them. The worst arguments happened when I was stressed by what was happening at work. That stress would lead me to drink too. Under those circumstances, it didn't take much for one or the other of us to say something hurtful. I never repeated my tactic of going for a long walk when I couldn't stand it anymore. But in a three-bedroom townhouse, I could end the conversation by going to a different room and shutting the door. One day when we were having one of these pointless arguments, Tony suddenly interrupted me.

"You think you're so smart, don't you. Well you're not. You probably even think I married you because I loved you."

That caught my attention. Telling me that I thought I was too smart was old news, but the line about why he married me was new. In the silence that followed his first statement, Tony threw his bombshell.

"There were several women I could have married; I picked you because you were the best source of income."

I turned on my heel and went out onto the deck where the air was clear and fresh. I never completely accepted that the only reason he married me was for my earning ability but it was devastating to hear him tell me that, even if it was only one of the reasons.

I had been aware for a while that the most important thing to me was really irrelevant to him. I wasn't pursuing a career to make money; I was pursuing a career because the intellectual challenge of my job made me happy. And Tony didn't understand that at all. He wasn't the first person, and wouldn't be the last, to say to me "you think too much." I could no more stop thinking than I could stop breathing. It was the need for intellectual stimulation that had driven me past all of the roadblocks that said "girls don't."

I had no idea how to fix my marriage. The right answer would have been to stop trying to fix it and just end it. But I wasn't ready to do that. I had been brought up to believe that you married for life. Divorce, while it was becoming more common, still had a stigma attached to it, and I had more status in society as a married woman than as a single woman. Plus I wasn't ready to admit that I had made such a serious mistake. Somehow the situation had to be fixable.

But I had a good idea about how to fix my job problem. I went looking for and found a job at Rand Information Systems as a programmer. They didn't need any more supervisors. So in the summer of 1973 when many people were glued to their TVs and radios listening to the Watergate hearings, I was moving on to a new and exciting chapter in my professional life.

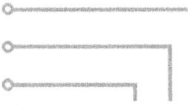

A New Job and
a New Home

WHEN I STARTED working for Rand Information Systems in June 1973, I was back to having a job where my talents and the needs of the organization meshed perfectly. "Randy" Rand had developed a niche market for the company and it was growing nicely. With the introduction of the IBM S/360, more organizations were moving from the older IBM machines to the IBM S/360 and were writing programs in COBOL. This created a need to convert an organization's existing programs, written in the Assembly Language of the old IBM machine, into COBOL. And Rand Information Systems was there to fill that need.

It was a purely technical job. You didn't need to know what the old program did; you just needed to make the converted version produce the same output that the original version did. The company had developed a translator program that took the old Assembly Language program as input and produced a COBOL program that everyone knew wasn't perfect. That was the job of the Rand programmer, to go through the old program line by line and fix everything the translator couldn't handle. Before hiring a new programmer, Rand gave applicants a test that was basically to fix a section of a program converted by the translator. I enjoyed the test and remember thinking that the people who were driving me crazy at the Sixth Army would not be able to do this work.

Since my talents and the job requirements meshed so well, I was happy and was quickly recognized as a valuable resource. The way I knew that they thought I was a valuable resource was that I was able to get two people hired at Rand after only being there for a few months. One of the hires was Dick P, a draftee programmer from the Sixth Army programming group who had worked for me for a while. Dick's enlistment was up and he had no desire to stay with the army so he was looking for a job. He passed the Rand test easily and moved on to the next step, the group interview. In this step a panel of three or four senior Rand programmers questioned the job candidate at length to see what he or she really knew and to make sure that passing the test wasn't a fluke. In Dick's case, however, after two or three questions, one of the programmers on the panel suggested they end the questions.

"Mary says this guy is what we are looking for. Why waste any more time, let's just hire him."

That vote of confidence made me feel good.

The other person I got hired at Rand was my sister Pat. Pat had graduated from college and gone on her own trip to Europe. After she came back, she started looking for a job in Seattle and wasn't having much luck. The job market seemed better in San Francisco so she moved in with us so she would have a place to stay while looking for a job. Our townhouse in Tiburon worked well for houseguests. The second floor was where the three bedrooms were. The master bedroom was on one side and the two guest bedrooms were on the other side. At the far end of the floor was a "Jack and Jill" bathroom. Two half baths with a bathtub/shower room in the middle. So Pat had a bedroom and a half bath all to herself with easy access to a tub.

Since I was happy with my job, I wasn't stressed. This meant that Tony and I weren't arguing while Pat lived with us. He may have even cut down on his drinking while she was there.

After a couple of months, when Pat hadn't found a job, I decided to see if I could get her a job at Rand. This had the potential to be a little difficult as Pat had no technical experience at all. But the company had a support group that did the preparation work for translations and testing. Programming skills were not a requirement for that group, and it saved programmer time for tasks that required programming skills. Because Pat was my sister, I was able to get her in the door for an interview even though she had no computer knowledge. And because she was Pat, she was able to convince them that her lack of technical knowledge was not a problem and she was hired. I'm not sure how much she admitted to the people at work but at first she really struggled with the weird vocabulary and acronyms that were part of the computer industry she found herself involved with.

Pat found an apartment in San Francisco on Balboa Street within walking distance of the office and moved into a place of her own. Since I helped her get the job at Rand, I will take some credit for her meeting her future husband Tom, who worked at Rand when Pat was hired.

One side effect of my going to work at Rand was that we had to buy a second car as we were no longer commuting together to the same office area. I liked the new Ford Pinto station wagon that had just come out. Since we weren't sure that it was a good long-term car for us, we ended up leasing it. This would actually work out well as when the lease ended we needed a bigger vehicle and didn't need to worry about selling the Pinto.

There was another advantage of my leaving the Sixth Army. I was able to cash out my government retirement account which provided us with a down payment to buy our first house. We still needed to get a loan from Mom and Dad to cover the closing costs of buying the house. This established the tradition of getting help with buying a house from "The Bank of Dad." All of my siblings used that source of funding over the years. Dad did make it clear that it was a loan, not a gift, and that he expected to be paid back in a timely fashion.

We had looked at houses in Tiburon while I was still working for the Sixth Army. We found one we really liked and could have afforded the mortgage payments but the banks were concerned about the sudden rise in the price of houses and wanted 20% down. We had no way to come up with even the 10% down that most house purchases required in those days much less 20%. It's a shame that we weren't in better financial shape as the house was only $60,000 in 1972 and I'm sure it is worth close to a million dollars today.

Eventually, in April 1974 we bought a house near the town of San Rafael, about ten miles north of Tiburon. It was still in Marin County but the commute to work was longer. The new house was in a subdivision built in the 1950s called Marinwood. When we turned off of Hwy 101 on to Lucas Valley Road, the first time we went to see the house, we thought we were in the country. But it was only one of the many green spaces that surrounded the area. We looked at a lot of houses before we saw our first "Eichler" house. Then we told our realtor that all we wanted to do was look at Eichler houses until we found the floor plan we wanted. Joseph Eichler was a real estate developer who built many post-World War II tract houses in the San Francisco Bay Area and in Southern California. Eichler homes are noted for their open floor plans and expansive windows. Both of us liked the house on Cedarberry Lane the moment we saw it. We became homeowners.

The house we bought had been a rental so there was work to do. A big expense was putting in new carpet throughout the house. As usual Tony and I argued about how much to spend. He wanted top of the line carpet. I wanted affordable carpet. The compromise was to limit the extravagant carpet to only the living room, the dining room, the family room and our bedroom. But it still blew our budget and caused problems initially paying back the loan to "The Bank of Dad." I was also successful in not buying a washer and dryer right away. After all, doing laundry was one of my chores. And I was willing to continue going to the laundromat until we could afford a washer and dryer. When we first married Tony and I had divided up chores as both of us were working. He hated doing laundry but was perfectly happy to defrost the freezer, a chore I hated doing. Of course, buying a new refrigerator was not optional with the new house and we got one with an automatic freezer defroster. After we bought a washer and dryer I came home one day to find Tony doing laundry.

"I thought you hated doing laundry?" I asked.

"Oh, no," Tony said, "I just hate going to laundromats."

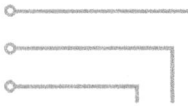

Diablo and Dante

IN EARLY 1975, Tony came home from work with the announcement that the United States Army had decided to close its programming unit in San Francisco. Tony, who was still working there, would not be fired but he would have to relocate to the east coast where his job was being moved as part of a consolidation of army functions. I was worried that we might have an argument about what to do next as I definitely didn't want to move east again. Fortunately, Tony had no interest in moving east either. Still, he was only forty-six, way too young to retire.

Tony's solution to being laid off was to make plans to start his own handyman business. He liked working with his hands and was quite handy around the house. He had spent some of his spare time building furniture and refinishing an old ornate table. The announcement of his plans included an additional idea. This would be a good time to get a dog. Just like I'd had dreams of going to the moon, Tony had always had dreams of getting a German Shepherd dog and naming him "Diablo." With his new business he would be working out of the house so he could take care of the dog during the day.

I'd grown up without pets. One of our houses in Bremerton had come with a cat, but it was a pretty independent outdoor cat and didn't really qualify as a pet as we didn't have to care for it. So I was rather uncomfortable around animals. I didn't know what to do with them.

But when Tony proposed getting a dog, I didn't really oppose it. After all, my track record of talking him out of doing things he wanted to do was pretty awful. But I did make it clear that it would be his dog and he would have to take care of it.

In September 1975 we went to a local breeder to meet Diablo, an eight-week-old German Shepherd puppy. It took me all of ten seconds to fall in love with this fifteen pounds of active fluff.

Since we got Diablo as a small puppy early in football season, we didn't want to leave him home alone all day on Sundays when we were tailgating and then watching the game. So we hired Tony's nephew Kurt to babysit Diablo during the football game. Tony made him a dog bed and we set it up on our covered back patio. When we were home during the day Diablo was allowed in the house, so we installed dog doors to allow him to go outside and then come back inside without our having to play doorman.

We took Diablo everywhere with us. Initially he rode in the car on my lap or at my feet in the seat well of the car. However, as he got bigger, I realized how much of a problem I had created. He quickly outgrew those places but didn't want to be anywhere else. We had to install a barrier to keep him out of the front seat of the car. Diablo might not have been trainable but I was. All subsequent puppies were not held on my lap and all rode in the back of the car.

It may have been that my growing up with siblings prompted my thought that Diablo should have a playmate. Or it may have been the fact that our puppy really enjoyed playing with the young boys across the street. And as Diablo got bigger the roughhousing with the boys got noisier. At first Tony was opposed to getting a second dog. He'd wanted one and he had that. Then one day he decided to agree with me.

"We could name him Dante." he said.

I was pleased that he'd come around to my point of view and was impressed by the cleverness of the name. Neither of us knew much Spanish, but we knew enough to know that Diablo meant "Devil." I would never have thought to put that tidbit of information together with the Italian author, Dante, who wrote *Inferno* about the seven circles of Hell. But that was what Tony had done.

Dante turned out to be a girl. The breeder we had gotten Diablo from suggested that a boy and a girl would be better than two boys. The two dogs had the same mother and were just a litter apart. So when Diablo was eight months old, he welcomed into his life, and ours, an eight-week-old Dante.

Tony built a second dog bed that was placed outside next to Diablo's dog bed. The new dog bed was slightly smaller. I guess Tony thought that Dante, as a girl, would be a smaller dog and thus would need a smaller dog bed.

The two dogs looked nothing alike as puppies. Diablo had been an all-black puppy, lightening, as he got older, to a black and tan dog. The breeder called Dante's color sable. It was a grayish-tan color that separated itself into a tan body with a gray saddle as she grew older.

The boys from across the street scared Dante with their loud, boisterous playing so they stopped coming over. That was fine with me. And Diablo had someone else to play with. We played fetch with the dogs because no one told us that German Shepherds didn't play fetch.

Because we bought our dogs from a breeder they had American Kennel Club registered names. This breeder had registered the dogs before we bought them. Diablo's registered name was "Quint" as he was part of the "Q" litter. Dante was registered as "Raspberry." She was a member of the "R" litter.

One drawback to getting a girl dog was that the breeder wanted a litter from her. This had the potential to cause problems as Diablo was a non-neutered male dog. Tony didn't believe in neutering male dogs. So when Dante was about six months old we took her back to the breeders for an examination. It turned out she had hip dysplasia. She had always had more trouble than Diablo getting into the car, but we had just assumed that because he was a boy he was more athletic. With hip dysplasia, Dante could not be bred. And the breeder said it was so bad that she needed to be put down. So with a heavy heart we surrendered our puppy to the breeder with the understanding that we could get the pick of the next litter that was about to be born.

About two months later I went back to the breeder to pick up the new puppy. While I was looking at the puppies, I saw a dog out of the corner of my eye.

It looked like Dante, but Dante was dead so I said, "I see you still have Rosemary," the name of the other female in Dante's litter.

"Oh, no," replied the breeder, "we decided to keep Raspberry." They always used Dante's registered name when talking about her.

"Give me my dog back," I insisted. I was irate and took her home to a long life with us.

Diablo and Dante

On weekends I took the dogs for walks at nearby Miller Creek Park. The park was named for the creek that ran through it. Our usual loop crossed the creek twice. The first crossing was at a low spot that could easily be forded. The second crossing was over a bridge. We were out for a walk one winter day and as I approached the fording area, I realized that recent rains had made the creek too high to ford. But the dogs were excited and just ran across it. Obviously they hadn't looked at the creek, because when I called them back to me, they were not the least bit interested in crossing the deep and fast running creek. So I started upstream towards the bridge and at first they followed me along the opposite bank. But after a short while they couldn't take it any longer and ran into the creek to come over to my side. At that point, the creek bed was about three or four feet below ground level and it was pretty steep. So I had to get down into the creek to help them up. Dante, who was used to being lifted into the car, helped me get her up out of the creek. Diablo thought he could be just dead weight. Fortunately, I convinced him to help me as there was no way I could lift a ninety-pound German Shepherd up a three-foot bank. I was probably wetter than if I'd forded the creek to be on the same side as the dogs.

Once we got dogs we started using our cabin in Dorrington more. The dogs loved having more room to roam, but they didn't go far. They would still stand by the door and ask me to take them for a walk. There was an unfortunate exception to that practice. One of the couples we knew from the Sixth Army, Vince and Gloria, had bought a cabin near ours, and the four of us started spending New Year's Eve at the cabins. Because Gloria had family that came up for the event, we went down to their house for dinner and cards and then champagne at midnight. We left the dogs in our cabin because they wanted to be part of the action and Vince and Gloria were not dog people. When we came home after midnight we put them outside and they slept near the cabin just like they slept near the house at home.

But one year when we got up on New Year's Day, there was no Diablo. We looked for him high and low for two days. We checked at the General Store in Dorrington in case someone had reported finding a dog. Without a phone at the cabin there was no point in putting up flyers as there was no way that anyone could get in touch with us. We tried to get Dante to track him, but that wasn't part of her skill set. Reluctantly we started to face the prospect of having to leave for home without him. We put together a flyer to post with our home phone number on it. Then we made one more trip to the General Store and there was a poster saying "German Shepherd found." It was Diablo. The people who found him said that he just lay on their back deck, which looked a lot like our back deck, and wouldn't move. He did eat and drink the food and water they provided for him. When we loaded him into the car, Dante beat him up. Someone had to and Tony and I were just so relieved to have him back.

A Detour into Management

Promoted Again

I'VE FORGOTTEN HOW we coped with only one paycheck after Tony left his job. Our modus operandi had pretty much been living paycheck to paycheck with two incomes. Tony did cash in his government retirement fund to help with the transition to one paycheck. He had plans for adding to the family income with his new business, but it really didn't take off.

Then I was approached at work about becoming a programming supervisor. The idea of promoting your best technical staff was still operating. The promotion would bring with it a good-sized pay raise. And there was one other appeal. As a supervisor I would have more input into how the company was run. If I stayed a technical person no matter how good I was, there were just some decisions where no one cared about your opinions about how the company operated.

135

So I accepted the promotion. Unlike the time I'd been a supervisor at the Sixth Army, I would be a working supervisor and still have technical work to do. So that was a plus. Still, it was the first time I'd wavered from my goal of having a career doing things that interested me. Computer programming was so much fun. I was learning new things constantly and finding ways to put concepts and techniques together in innovative and more effective ways. I especially loved the problem-solving aspects of the job and the satisfaction of knowing when I'd solved the problem. A non-working program suddenly worked.

Being a supervisor meant I had to spend more time dealing with the ambiguities of people. It was a useful skill to learn but not anything I particularly enjoyed doing. But there was the appeal of more money and I liked the idea of having a voice in how the company was run. The fact that so few women were being promoted in those days was also a factor. Did it really make sense to turn down a promotion when women supervisors were so rare?

The reason they were looking for a new supervisor was that the company was growing. For a while we had moved our expanding work force into more empty spaces in the partially residential, partially commercial area on Geary Blvd near Arguello Blvd. But eventually that was no longer a viable option for the organization. So a search was started to find a suitable space downtown. The lease for a building on Battery Street had been signed before I was promoted, but I was involved in the allocation of space in the new building.

About this time, the company was also starting to expand overseas. Unlike most people I wasn't thrilled with overseas work. What we did was hard enough to do well without having to deal with language differences. But when a contract with a company in London was finalized, I volunteered to manage that one. I was quickly reminded of my trip to Europe several years earlier when I had to deal with a slightly different version of English. Usually once a day when I was in London talking to the British project manager, one or the other of us would say something that the other one didn't understand. And then the speaker would rephrase the statement without using idioms. It was educational.

Unfortunately, the company's growth didn't continue, and for the first time ever, the company had to resort to layoffs. There were two rounds. Senior management decided who to layoff in the first round. I had to tell people that they were being let go. In the second round, which was tougher as some good people were let go, I was part of the decision-making process. To this day, I'm not sure whether it was easier to be part of the decision-making process or not.

My future brother-in-law, Tom, was let go in the first round. He was part of our administrative staff and at first was not selected to be laid off. But he went to the Human Resources Department and convinced them to lay him off rather than the original selectee, a single mother with a small child. For years I was overwhelmingly impressed with Tom's action. Then many years later, he told me he just wanted to be laid off so he could collect unemployment insurance.

I'm not sure I believe that unemployment insurance was his only motivation. He did go on to a long career in the non-profit sector.

My problems being a supervisor continued. I had no experience, little natural talent in that area and no guidance. One of my biggest problems was balancing doing the work I enjoyed doing with the supervisory work that I was struggling with. And my overall performance suffered. I wasn't sure I could financially afford to go back to just being a programmer, plus there were aspects of being part of management that I liked.

Fortunately the company's fortunes started to improve so I didn't have to worry about being let go in the next round of layoffs. What saved both the company and me was that the company expanded into a new line of work. We were now designing Order Entry Systems for Fortune 200 companies. This market opportunity opened up because it was now possible to attach remote terminals to computers and information could be entered directly into the computer from remote sites rather than being written down on paper forms for later data entry. Large companies wanted to change their systems to make use of the new technology.

The new head of marketing, who had been an employee of a large computer company, brought with him a discontinued prototype project. This allowed Rand Information Systems to move into this new line of work. We also acquired some of the staff that had worked on the prototype project to help us get started. One of the new people, Ed, did some recruiting among existing Rand staff. He was starting a project to design and possibly build an Order Entry System for a large pharmaceutical company, Abbott Laboratories, and needed staff. I was his first recruit.

Becoming a Designer

WHEN I JOINED the new Order Entry System development group in 1976, I acquired a mentor for the first time in my career. I didn't know anything about Order Entry Systems even though that was what the group I'd worked for at the Sixth Army did. But Ed knew Order Entry well. He was also a trained manager and was willing to teach me about management too. My natural curiosity and analytical ability were what he needed on the project. A trained Order Entry System developer would have been his first choice, but turning me into one was a viable option.

After years of avoiding learning about the business behind the projects I was working on, I was pleasantly surprised to find out that business systems, whether computerized or not, could be fascinating. My first project with Ed was to develop a Functional Specification, basically a high level design, for Abbott Laboratories' new Order Entry System. There was a starting generic document that we had to modify to reflect what made Abbott's business different. It was fascinating to watch Ed question the Abbott people to understand how their Order Entry process worked and how it needed to be changed to make it better. Ed was about fifty. He wasn't an imposing looking man, a little on the short side, not much taller than I was. But he had such a self-confident manner about him when he spoke that the Abbott people listened. Over the years of being the new kid in school, I'd mastered the art of blending in until I got the lay of the land. Now, watching Ed, I was learning a different way of approaching a new group of people.

In one information gathering session, an Abbott person grumbled to us.

"It's silly to hire you to do the design when we're the ones with all of the knowledge."

I used my observation of what Ed was doing to reply.

"But we know the first fifty questions to ask to get the project really started."

Ed later told me that it was the best description of a consultant he'd ever heard.

The Abbott Functional Specification project took three months to complete. We alternated between spending a week at the client site gathering information and two weeks in the office documenting what we had learned. Our finished document was about seventy pages. Producing and revising it in two weeks was only possible because Rand had just moved from having secretarial support with typewriters to having a word processing department. Instead of creatively modifying documents so that multiple pages didn't have to be retyped to make a simple change, it was now possible to just make the needed changes and have the word processing software take care of reformatting and printing. With a word processing department, we still had to handwrite the original document on lined paper and mark small changes on the printed document. But as we were running out of time near the end of the project, I would occasionally take over a word processing terminal and make the changes to the document myself. It was faster. By the end of my next project, I had a word processing terminal in my office and the phase-out of the word processing department had begun.

Ed taught me about Order Entry systems and project management after work when we were at the client's site. We also had time for instruction while the word process-ing department was producing our document. Ed had the luxury of only working on one project and it gave me a rare opportunity to learn new skills. We also had time for social conversation. I was surprised to find out that Ed and his wife had met when they were ballet dancers. People follow interesting paths to their careers.

Writing the Functional Specification for Abbott's new system was basically paid marketing. It allowed us to gather enough information to put a fixed price on the design phase of the project and estimate the development costs. Abbott Labs was not ready to sign a contract with us to move to the next phase so that project went on hold. However, there was a new project that was starting. This one was to develop the Functional Specification for Sun Oil's new Order Entry System. Ed got promoted to department manager, and I was assigned as the project manager for the new Sun Oil project. I would still be working for Ed so he could continue to teach me what I needed to know to do that job. I also acquired another mentor.

Marshall was assigned as my assistant to develop the Functional Specification. He was an experienced marketing man, with experience in management and systems development. As he was over sixty and approaching retirement, he wasn't interested in managing another large project. But he was a great person to become the other half of my team. He was generous in sharing what he knew and so, in spite of my still limited knowledge and systems development experience, we completed the Functional Specification and Sun Oil signed a contract with Rand to develop their new Order Entry System. The Sun Oil Functional Specification study wasn't as intense as the Abbott study had been because I knew more at the start of the project. This meant that Marshall and I had more time for social conversations when on-site. We tended to talk about dogs. He had Borzois and was a dog show judge.

Most people don't start their business systems development career managing a million dollar development project and the Sun Oil project would have been a multi-million dollar project in today's dollars. But Ed, having placed me in the job, provided me with lots of management help. And

Sun Oil appointed Joe, an experienced project manager, to run the overall project. In addition to a willingness to learn, I brought to the effort a complete understanding of the design and a lot of programming experience. It wasn't until much later that I appreciated how instrumental Joe had been in our success. He understood that our success was important to the project's success and was willing to give a little in negotiations with his vendor, us, rather than always insisting on doing things his way.

But even with all the help I got, I received the credit. In late 1978 our new company president, Dale, handed out a series of awards. They were engraved sterling silver bowls. In spite of the fact that we were still in the development phase of the Sun Oil project, I got the award for Project Manager of the Year. Ed received the Department Manager of the Year award.

I acquired one more skill during those first two projects. I learned how to write again. It had been over ten years since I had written anything and my writing skills had deteriorated. Both Ed and Marshall knew how to write technical documents and made sure that the Functional Specification for the Abbott and Sun projects were well written even if I did much of the writing. And Dick, who was Ed's boss, looked in horror at my first status report memo.

"What are you trying to say?" he asked.

After I told him, he said, "Why don't you say that?"

He then spent time working on my written communication skills. There were some definite advantages of working for a small company that had brought in outside expertise to be its management team.

***

The work I was now doing required a lot of business travel. During the early phases of projects I was spending a third of my time at the client site. In the later phases it was sometimes up to 25% of my time. The good thing about the business travel was that it got me away from home.

After Tony became an independent contractor, he had started to drink more. One of the reasons his contracting business didn't take off was because of his drinking. I suspected this and had it confirmed by my coworker, Marshall. I had been advertising Tony's services to people at Rand, and Marshall, who had been on the Sun project with me, had hired him to do some work. I found out later from Marshall that Tony hadn't finished the work because of his drinking, and Marshall had had to hire someone else to finish the job. I was embarrassed and apologized.

"It's not your fault." Marshall said, "But I thought you should know."

When I asked Tony about it, he denied not finishing the job. He made some comment about clients who were too picky. I let it go. I'd given up arguing with him. He'd learned too well how to push my buttons and make me angry. I did stop suggesting people I knew hire Tony to do work for them.

The additional problem with Tony's increased drinking was that when I was home, I was drinking more too. I didn't have that problem when I was on the road. After eight years of a problematic marriage, I was finally willing to admit to myself that I'd made a mistake in marrying Tony. But, for the moment, ignoring the problem was the easiest thing to do.

The other advantage of business travel was that during the second year of the Sun project I got to spend more time with my sister Maggie. She had started working for Uncle Carl's company, G&H, as a technical writer in December 1977 after she returned from her around-the-world jaunt as a teacher. After she graduated from college, Maggie had obtained a job as a teacher on Guam and after that contract was up, she began her trip home by going to Europe. She stopped in Greece and liked it so much that she wanted to stay. However, she couldn't find a job in Greece that paid enough to live on. All she could find were substitute teacher jobs. So she moved on to Germany where she got a job teaching soldiers. Eventually she returned home and began looking for a writing job.

In January 1978, after a month of training in Chicago, she started her job in G&H's Philadelphia office. The Sun Oil department I was working with had its offices in Philadelphia. We did a few things together during 1978 when I was on site in Philadelphia, but she was living in New Jersey and commuted to the office that year. Then in January 1979, she moved into Center City Philadelphia. It worked out well for us. As part of an ongoing project I was paid a per diem, rather than actual expenses. So I stayed with Maggie and spent the money I would have spent on a hotel on nice dinners for the two of us. Maggie was also my guide to Center City, which had received a substantial facelift during Philadelphia's preparations for the Bicentennial celebrations in 1976. I had missed all of the celebrations as the Sun project didn't start until the fall of 1976.

***

As the Sun project was finishing up, the Abbott project came back to life. With the Sun project having been successful and with my having worked on the Abbott Functional Specification, it made sense for me to manage the Abbott project. We began design work in the winter of 1979-1980 during a major stretch of snowstorms in the Midwest. North Chicago, where Abbott was headquartered, got more than its share of snow. Streets were lined with eight- to ten-feet-high snowbanks and driving was a definite challenge. By the time we finished the design and started development work, the snow had melted and none of us recognized the area any more.

The design for the Abbott Order Entry System was functionally different from the Sun Oil Order Entry System. This was mostly because Abbott was a pharmaceutical company and Sun was an oil company. There was also a big technical difference between the two systems. At that time there were two database systems in use, IMS and IDMS. All of our previous systems, including the Sun system, had used IMS. But all of Abbott's existing systems used IDMS and they wanted their Order Entry System to use the same type of databases. All of our existing programmers knew IMS and none of them knew IDMS. Plus there were many more IMS programmers in the area than there were IDMS programmers so we couldn't hire our way out of the problem. We had to train existing programmers to use IDMS databases. The cost of our system development effort was a big impediment to selling the Abbott system. Senior management decided we couldn't include the cost of training in our price. I wasn't experienced enough to negotiate a separate budget for me with my management that included training time so I started the project with a plan that I knew was going to be over budget. I established this plan because I knew that it was cheaper to spend the time formally training project staff rather than just pretending that they would acquire the new knowledge on their own.

By the mid-1970s new technology was changing the way programs were created. Instead of the old method of coding a program on coding sheets and having them keypunched, programmers were starting to use terminals to connect to our computer and create their own programs. At first there was a terminal room for programmers to use. Initially the room contained terminals that were referred to as "line at a time" terminals. Each line on the screen was printed sequentially and as the screen filled up, the top lines disappeared. These terminals had a data entry line at the bottom of the screen. They worked fine for creating programs.

The Order Entry systems we were building used IBM 3270 terminals that were referred to as "full screen" terminals. Basically the screen was a form to fill out. Hitting the "enter" key sent all of the data on the screen to the computer at one time. These terminals were needed to test the systems as they were being built. Since IBM 3270 terminals could also be used to create programs, we gradually replaced all of the "line at a time" terminals with "full screen" IBM 3270 terminals. Neither of these terminal types had flat screens; they both had big bulky CRT screens.

By the time the Abbott project was fully staffed, we had one IBM 3270 terminal in each cubicle for two programmers to share. The terminal was placed on a short desk area between the two programmers. It could be turned to face either person as required. We thought we were so technically advanced.

***

While I was advancing my career, allowing dogs into my life and struggling with the value of my marriage, the rest of the world was busy spinning on its own axis.

The family was growing in size. Pat and Tom got married in September 1977. I received the only written invitation to their wedding. Pat and I were both still working at Rand, and she wrote a note on the desk calendar in my office. It said something like "It's happening about 2 p.m. on Saturday."

My brother John married Candice in April 1978. Their wedding was as formal as Pat and Tom's had been casual. All of the wedding party, which included brother Chris as the best man and Candice's daughter Beth, were dressed in white. Beth was Mom and Dad's first grandchild. Pat presented them with their first biological grandchild when Rob was born the following year.

Before John married Candice, he had sailed aboard the *Glomar Challenger* helping to map the floor of the oceans. While he was doing this work, he became the first of the siblings to go around the world. Not much later, Maggie matched this milestone when she returned from Guam with stops in Europe.

Like everyone else we waited in gas lines in 1973. The most insightful economic statement I remember was "there was a shortage of gas that cost less than a dollar. There was lots of gas that cost more than a dollar." California had one of its periodic droughts in 1976 and 1977. This one was bad enough that mandatory water rationing was imposed. Even with the water rationing, Marin County, where we lived, was in danger of running out of water. A pipeline was built across the Richmond-San Rafael Bridge to supply the county with more water.

On the lighter side of things, it looked like 49ers football games were about to improve. For a couple of years in the late 1970s, we talked about just having tailgate parties and not bothering to watch the football game as the team was losing most of the time. Then in 1979, the 49ers hired Bill Walsh to be their head coach and Bill drafted Joe Montana and Dwight Clark. The first year of the era of the "West Coast Offense" was about the same as the previous year, but things were about to get a lot better.

Zero Seven Charlie

MY PRIVATE PILOT days seemed to come to an end in the early 1970s. There were too many other things that seemed more important and after we bought the house, the expense of flying was not in the budget at all. However, we still maintained our membership in the Aircraft Owners and Pilots Association (AOPA). Their monthly magazine was fun to read and provided memories of simpler days when I had been younger. In late 1979, Tony read an article in the AOPA magazine about the benefits of buying a plane and leasing it to a flying club. One of the advantages of this plan was that the cost of flying lessons was included in the price of the airplane. With plenty of time on his hands, as his handyman business was more of an idea than reality, Tony decided that learning to fly would be a good thing for him to do. He did some research on this program and found that the closest airport where we could buy a plane and lease it back was in Santa Rosa, about forty minutes north of us. After talking to the operator of the private airplane portion of the airport, Tony let me know that getting my pilot license current again would be included in the deal.

Given Tony's track record of talking me into things that seemed reasonable but that we ended up not being able to afford, I should have been more cautious. But I did want to resume flying. And there were fewer and fewer things that Tony and I did together. Having just celebrated our tenth wedding anniversary, I thought it was worth one more try to make our marriage work by finding something new that we could do together. I also knew he couldn't fly and drink.

So I went along with the idea of buying a plane even though the thing that made it "affordable" was a huge tax gimmick. Since we had no savings and I knew that there would be unexpected expenses, we tapped the equity in our house to create a small contingency fund. Unfortunately, we needed to use some of this money right away. On my first lesson to get my license current again, I drove the plane off of the runway and nicked the propeller on one of the runway lights. The propeller could not be fixed and it cost about $1000 to replace it. Ouch. The collision with the runway light demonstrated two things. The first was how rusty my piloting skills were. The second was how aviation had changed since I'd started flying. The reason I ran off the runway and into the runway light was that I became confused while talking to ground control and taxiing the plane at the same time. When I had learned to fly and even while flying out of Hamilton AFB, the last airport I'd flown out of, talking on the radio during a flight and on the ground was a pretty infrequent thing, so I never really learned how to do it well when I was learning to fly. But now skill in using a radio was required if you were going to fly.

We bought a Piper Cherokee 180. It carried four people and had room for luggage. It came with the registration number of N4507C. But when identifying yourself while flying, only the last three characters of the number were used. So we became Zero Seven Charlie. Charlie was aviation speak for the letter "C." The plane had a basic instrumentation panel but since that was all I was capable of using, it worked fine for us. Except for being a little longer, it looked a lot like the Cherokee 140 I'd learned to fly in. It was even the same color—white with a red stripe.

The plan was for me to take enough lessons to get my license current again and then fly the plane up to Bremerton for a trip to visit my family. Upon our return, Zero Seven Charlie would become part of the planes used by the Sonoma Valley Flyers. And we would be paid when pilots without their own planes used ours. Then Tony would begin his lessons during times when the plane wasn't being rented by others. It seemed pretty straightforward at the time.

The instructor turned me loose to fly on my own too soon as I had one other minor mishap before heading off to Bremerton. In spite of its cost, the damaged propeller was a minor accident as no one was endangered. My second mishap was to apply the brakes too early on a landing. As a result the wheels were locked when I touched down and the plane skidded off the runway. Fortunately I did this away from the Santa Rosa airport at the small airport in Cloverdale and only skidded onto the dirt beside the runway. Other than my pride, nothing was damaged and I didn't bother to tell anyone.

Even with my rocky start, I felt comfortable being a pilot as we headed north to Kitsap International Airport, a small airport just outside of Bremerton. This was in 1980, the summer I turned thirty-six. Months earlier Mount St. Helens had erupted and everyone we knew in California was concerned that we would be flying near the volcano. My stock response was that we would be at least one hundred miles away and so I would have time to get the plane on the ground before the blast would get to us. I'm not sure I was quite that confident but felt the odds were not high for another eruption. As soon as we got to Bremerton, the question changed to, "Are we going to fly to Mount St. Helens and look at it?"

Zero Seven Charlie didn't carry enough fuel to fly from the Santa Rosa Airport to Kitsap International Airport so we made a stop en route. On the flight north I carefully plotted out a straight-line course to our fueling stop in Roseburg, Oregon, and then from Roseburg to Kitsap International Airport. I picked Roseburg because of its mid-flight location and the fact that it didn't have tower controlled landings. I hadn't done enough flying using the radio to be really comfortable with the radio yet. The landing at Roseburg ranks among my worst landings. I flared out a foot or so above the ground so we landed hard. It even put a crack in the fiberglass faring over the right wheel. But it was still a landing we walked away from and after filling up the tank and getting some lunch we continued on our way. The landing at Kitsap International Airport was uneventful. Dad and other family members were there to see the plane and drive us to Bremerton.

The flight to see Mount St. Helens was unsuccessful. There was a no-fly zone around the mountain, but we didn't even get close to that. As we approached the mountain, the unsettled air bounced the plane around so much that I had no desire to go any closer. The volcano was making its own weather and it was turbulent.

My passengers on the flight were Gram and Chris. Chris told me that one of the more interesting parts of the flight was the landing back at Kitsap International Airport.

"You were casual for most of the flight," he said, "And then as the landing began, you suddenly became intense. Or maybe focused is a better word."

I wasn't aware of the change but it made sense. The trickiest part of any flight is the landing.

The day we were to head back home to California was very overcast. The ceiling, the bottom of the clouds, was only a few thousand feet. As I was only licensed for visual flight rules, I had to fly below the clouds so I could see where I was going. Under normal circumstances, we would have just postponed the flight home by a day. I could have taken another vacation day and Tony wasn't working. But he had an appointment and didn't want to miss it. So we headed out with marginal weather. This time I didn't draw our flight plan as a straight line. On the flight up I realized how easy it would be to just follow I-5 so that is what we did. The low ceiling made flying a little uncomfortable as we were closer to the ground than I was used to. And it didn't seem to be getting better. We made a stop at a small airport just across the Oregon border to check the weather. The clouds were thinning further south so we pressed on and fairly soon after that were able to climb to a more normal cruising altitude of about five thousand feet. Our refueling stop on the way home was in Medford, Oregon. It was a tower controlled airport, but I'd gotten much more confident with my radio skills with all of the flying I had done since leaving Santa Rosa. It was a good landing in Medford and an excellent landing back home in Santa Rosa.

I'd enjoyed the flight and was delighted with how my piloting skills had returned with practice. It was unfortunately to be the only long flight of my piloting career. Once we returned home we began leasing out the plane.

Things didn't go as planned. We weren't making as much money as we had expected by leasing out the plane. The economy was in a downturn and people were flying less. Tony wasn't interested in going up and taking lessons during the week on his own, and I had no interest in going and hanging out while he was taking lessons. I wanted to keep my skills current and to go places. He wanted a supportive wife. I wanted a partner to do things with. Neither of us was happy with what we had and neither of us was willing to change. My hopes of finding something we could do together didn't happen. We continued our routine of not talking about problems and leading separate lives.

As a result, we weren't getting too much use out of the plane. But there were still monthly bills to pay for the plane and the second mortgage we had acquired. So after about two years we, or probably just me, decided to sell the plane. The trouble with this decision was that because it was a tax gimmick that made the financial numbers appealing, we got hit with a huge tax penalty. A refinancing of our second mortgage got us through that crisis but for the first time we had a big debt that wasn't the result of acquiring something or improving the quality of our life. It would be many years before I finally had the financial situation back under control but this was to be our last extravagance.

Winning the Drawings

WE MADE TWO other unusual trips in the early 1980s. In June 1981 and again in January 1982 we won trips as a result of random drawings. Sometimes you get lucky. One trip was more fun than the other but the other trip was something you could brag about forever.

In early 1981 we made a contribution to the San Francisco Symphony. In June we received a notice that we had won the Mississippi River Cruise. The cruise was to leave New Orleans the evening of Friday, November 20, 1981, and return the morning of Friday, November 27, 1981, so we had lots of time to plan the trip and to look forward to it.

We left the San Francisco airport early Friday morning on our way to New Orleans. We arrived in plenty of time to board the steamboat *Mississippi Queen* by 5 p.m. and start our cruise. Our cabin was a deluxe veranda stateroom. Not a suite but on the nicer end of cabins available. Dinner that night was a buffet and then there was music and dancing. While we were occupied with the Dixieland music, the steamboat left the dock and we were on our way.

Most of the first day of the cruise was spent moving up river. We made a stop to visit the first of the many pre-Civil War homes we would tour on the trip. I learned that just because you had seen one antebellum mansion, as these homes were usually referred to, you hadn't really seen much of the style of the period. We ended the day with music and dancing in the Grand Salon. This routine of tours during the day and music and dancing at night would become the pattern for the rest of the trip.

Sunday morning found us docked in St. Francisville. The description of the town begins with "In the mid-1880s fully half of the millionaires in America lived in the West Feliciana Parish of Louisiana." The Rosedown Plantation and Gardens and the Myrtles plantation home that we visited reflected the wealth that this area had once had.

We cruised on the river all day Monday. I did manage, in spite of my limited musical skills, to acquire a notice that I was a duly certified calliopist having played something recognizable on the ship's calliope. There were also bridge and bingo games to keep passengers occupied. Plus music and drinking. The drink of the day on Monday was a Scarlet O'Hara, made with cranberry juice, lime juice and Southern Comfort. I passed on that one. Drinks on the cruise were cheap and name brands were only ten cents more than stock brands so I used my drinking time to consume Johnny Walker Black, my choice of a first-class scotch.

We spent all of Tuesday at Vicksburg. In addition to the tour of the battlefield, we also visited the Court House Museum and three more antebellum houses. I probably should have taken the hiking tour of the battlefield even if it meant missing the house tours. After having hiked so many east coast Civil War battlefields, I was disappointed with the bus tour. However, the sunken Civil War ship, the USS *Cairo*, which had been raised from the riverbed and was being restored, was interesting. The USS *Cairo* was one of the ironclad ships used by the South during the Civil War which was called "The War Between the States" on all the material I saw during the cruise.

Back on the *Mississippi Queen*, there was a tour of the pilot house. Having been on many ships because of my navy brat background, I was initially perplexed by the lack of a compass in the pilot house. But the Captain's wife, who was giving the tour, assured me that a compass wasn't needed.

"With all the bends in the river, a compass is of no use on a river boat. The pilot has to know which way he is going by using landmarks," she said.

Unlike our other stops on the river, at Vicksburg we were docked off the main part of the river and it was fascinating to watch the pilot turn the boat around in a body of water not much wider than the length of the boat.

We headed south after Vicksburg and Wednesday morning found us in Natchez. The town is on a high bluff above the river and was one of the few southern cities not extensively damaged by the Civil War. As a result there are over two hundred antebellum homes in Natchez, and we toured four of them including Longwood which was unfinished at the start of the war and remains in that state today. The other interesting thing that happened that day was that the *Delta Queen*, the sister ship of our vessel, tied up alongside of us in the afternoon. It was interesting to tour as, unlike the modern *Mississippi Queen*, the *Delta Queen* had been a working paddle wheeler taking passengers and goods between Sacramento and San Francisco in the 1920s and 1930s. With the short winter days, it was after dark before the *Delta Queen* left our side and we were underway shortly after that.

I'm leaving the Mississippi Queen during our stop in Vicksburg

We were still cruising when we woke up Thanksgiving morning. The tour of the engine room that morning wasn't publicized to keep attendance low but, if you were an old hand at ships like me, and knew to ask, you knew when it was happening. Like most engine rooms, it was very noisy.

We arrived at Nottoway Plantation, the largest plantation home in the South, about noon. It was our last tour of the cruise and like all of the other tours on the cruise, I went by myself. Tony had no interest. Or perhaps the physical problems that were starting to appear because of his drinking may have made him unwilling to do anything that required him to walk any distance. He was starting to get shaky. Occasionally he would grab my arm for support when we were walking. At the buffet meals on the cruise he would ask me to get something for him because he was having trouble holding a tray. One area though where he didn't seem to have any physical limitations was dancing. Tony was an excellent dancer and competitive. I was a terrible dancer, although if Tony was leading well, I could follow well enough to look like I knew what I was doing. There was another couple on the cruise that were good dancers and enjoyed showing off their dancing skills. Tony's competitive spirit kicked in and he wanted to show off his dancing skills as well. Unfortunately, I was his partner and so he was as frustrated during the nightly dance events on the cruise as I was during the daily tours. It was like we were on two different cruises. Still I enjoyed the trip. I'm not sure he did.

We didn't talk about the trip after it was over. We weren't talking about much in those days.

Since Thursday was the last day of the cruise, lots of pictures of people, both staff and other passengers, were taken before, during and after Thanksgiving dinner. There was traditional turkey with all the fixings but nontraditional people could order ham or roast beef. We also had to pack that night as the cruise was over at 9 a.m. on Friday.

We didn't have far to go after leaving the *Mississippi Queen* Friday morning as we had made reservations at the Hilton Hotel on the river. Our room overlooked the river so we were able to watch "our" boat as it departed on its next cruise at 9 p.m. that night. Saturday was devoted to touring New Orleans. Our first stop was Brennan's, a restaurant famous for its breakfasts. The great food we had enjoyed on the cruise continued in New Orleans.

Sunday morning we went to the airport for our flight home. It was time to return to our normal life. Tony's parents, who believed that dogs were outside pets, had stayed at our house while we were gone to take care of the dogs. Diablo and Dante were glad to have us home.

***

The second trip we took that winter was to Super Bowl XVI. It gave us bragging rights forever among football fans. We were there when the 49ers won their first Super Bowl.

We had become 49ers season ticket holders in 1971 when the 49ers moved their home field to Candlestick Park. Tony's sister Rosemary and her husband Howard also got season tickets that year. During the years when the team was awful, there was sometimes discussion about not bothering to go to the game but we always did go. We referred to ourselves as the "49er Faithful." Then came the 1981 season. No one was expecting much as the team had lost ten games and only won six games the year before. But with the new passing threat of Joe Montana to Dwight Clarke, they started winning. And for the first time since I'd been a 49ers fan, they beat Dallas in the playoffs and that meant they were in the Super Bowl. I think the team management was also caught by surprise. They didn't realize they could make lots of money from Super Bowl tickets and put most of the tickets into a lottery for the season ticket holders. We got tickets. Howard and Rosemary got tickets. The four of us made plans to go to Detroit for Super Bowl XVI. This was the first year that the NFL held the Super Bowl in a cold, snowy area of the country, but Detroit had an indoor stadium and the weather wouldn't be a factor during the game.

We got a package deal. A charter flight to Detroit, a hotel overnight, bus rides to the hotel, the game and the airport after the game and, of course, the flight home. There was even a pep rally scheduled before the game. It was one of the most exciting competitive Super Bowls up to that time. The 49ers won 26-21, but they had to mount an impressive goal line defense to prevent the Cincinnati Bengals from scoring the winning touchdown.

One of the more amazing things about the game didn't happen on the field but in the stands. The two seats next to us were not used. It was nice to have a place to stash our coats, but you had to wonder who those seats belonged to and why they hadn't made the game.

The trip home was surprisingly dull. At first everyone was excited. We had won! But the organizers of the charter flight had limited drinks on the plane to only two per person so there was no rowdy celebration. And most people had to get up the next morning and go to work. I wasn't the only one who realized they were tired. We'd managed to cram a lot into the weekend.

After it was over, I was glad I had gone, but I would be perfectly happy never to go to another Super Bowl. I missed watching the game from our regular seats. I missed the group that sat in the adjoining seats. And while the game itself was enjoyable, there was something too sterile and regimented about the organized part of the trip. Still, both Tony and I had enjoyed the trip and that was a good thing.

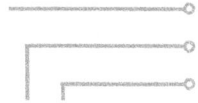

A Promotion Too Far

R AND INFORMATION SYSTEMS, the company I was working for, was growing too fast again. Too much of the management structure was being staffed by inexperienced people. And I was one of them. My strength as a project manager was that I understood the design of the system we were building and as questions came up I could make decisions that kept the integrity of the design in place. I also understood the critical paths of the project. I had been able to keep my first project, the one for Sun Oil, running smoothly with just these two skills because I had a lot of help from Joe, the Sun project manager, and my boss, Ed, on the other aspects of project management.

My second project for Abbott Laboratories was a bigger, more complex project which might have been okay as I now had more experience. But without the help from Ed, who now had many other things to worry about, and with the Abbott project manager being less helpful than the Sun project manager, I was constantly being sideswiped by issues that Joe and Ed had helped resolve on my last project.

Part of the reason Ed was so busy is that our marketing department was selling as much as they could. And since we were selling development projects, no client was going to sign on the dotted line until they had met the technical manager who was going to be responsible for the project. For a long time that had been Ed. But he was stretched too thin. The solution was to promote me to project director. This meant that in addition to my job of managing the Abbott project, I was to provide technical support to our salesmen and be the responsible technical manager that the client could believe in.

On paper the Abbott project was going well and I had two good team leaders who were doing the day-to-day management of the programmers. Plus I liked front-end design work more than doing day-to-day management, so I was easy to convince that I could do both jobs. Of course, I couldn't, and the Abbott project got into more trouble than I was capable of getting it out of. Fortunately because we were a small company, the senior people running the company had the management and marketing experience I lacked and were able to negotiate our way out of the problem.

It's not clear that if I had remained a full-time project manager, the project wouldn't have gotten into trouble anyway, but I like to think that the chances were less. The source of the biggest problem was work that was done by the client staff that didn't follow our specs, and by the time I realized the nature of the problem, it was too late to use that material and a plan B had to be developed. If I'd been working on the project full time, I suspect I would have spotted the problem much sooner. From a financial point of view, the Abbot project was completed in good shape. But unlike Sun, who would be a good reference for us, Abbott would only be a marginal one.

Even with problems though, the Abbott project was one of the better projects going on. We were selling too many projects for the amount of trained staff we had and sooner or later that would impact the quality of our delivered product. I think Ed saw the writing on the wall and decided to retire. Ed had had two project directors working for him, John F and me. Senior management decided that the best way to keep us both at the company was to divide Ed's department into two pieces and give one piece to each of us. I think they were concerned that whoever wasn't promoted would quit. They may have been right. John had worked for me briefly on a small standalone piece of one of my projects. It was a temporary assignment as he had some free time and I needed help. However, I quickly discovered the best way to work with him was just to leave him alone. It worked fine for that short assignment. I'm not sure how well it would have worked long term.

So I became department manager for all of our east coast projects. This increased the amount of time I spent visiting clients and potential clients. One year, either 1981 or 1982, I made twenty-three trips to the east coast. Many of these trips were short, only two or three days, but I did perfect the 23-hour trip to Boston which began by mistake. I had to go to Boston for a marketing meeting and just didn't have two days to devote to the trip. So being young and indestructible then, I caught a red-eye flight out of San Francisco at 10 p.m., got some sleep on the plane, attended the meeting and caught a flight home that landed in San Francisco at 9 p.m. I decided I was no more tired on this schedule than flying into Boston the night before and getting a partial night's sleep because of the time difference. So I added this flight plan to my schedule. I may have claimed I was awake for all of these meetings but I wonder how well I was really functioning. I remember one moment when I was sitting on a plane in an airport and for a moment couldn't remember where I was or what I was doing there. I shrugged it off, but it was a clear indication of the stress I was under.

The department manager in her window office

My promotion to department manager was a mistake. I was totally incapable of doing the job. It was a classic case of the Peter Principle: "In a hierarchy every employee tends to rise to his level of incompetence." This management concept was described by Laurence J. Peters in *The Peter Principle* that was published in 1968.

There were, however, parts of the job I could do well. Before I crashed and burned, I did accomplish two things that I added as imaginary trophies on my imaginary fireplace mantle.

Over the course of my life, I have received a number of awards. There were Girl Scout merit badges, tennis trophies, pieces of paper either framed or suitable for framing, assorted plaques and even the engraved silver bowl I received during the Sun project. But my most treasured awards are the non-physical ones. These awards came from a compliment given to me by someone after I'd done something I was particularly proud of. I think of these as my imaginary trophies on my imaginary fireplace mantle.

Kelly, one of the senior Rand programmers, gave me my favorite imaginary trophy.

"When we organize the programmers into a union," he said, "I want you to negotiate with management for us."

Now I knew that I wasn't really the negotiator he would want, but his words expressed appreciation for my accomplishing something we both knew was important and, at first glance, seemed impossible to achieve.

That accomplishment began one day when Dan H, one of the programmers who worked for me, came into my office with news.

"I like working here," he said. "I don't want to leave, but I've just been offered a job paying twenty-five percent more than I'm being paid now."

After a pause, he continued. "I know I'm due for a pay raise soon but I also know there is no way you can match that offer. It's a lot of money. I feel like I have to take it."

I knew two things. The first was that Dan was worth every penny the other company was willing to pay him. The second was that he was an employee we didn't want to lose. I needed to do something.

"Will you give me twenty-four hours before doing anything?" I asked.

He said yes, expecting, of course, that I wouldn't be able to do anything, and I had my task set out before me.

First let me explain how Dan got so underpaid. The company had tried to deal with the runaway inflation of the late 1970s and early 1980s by increasing the size of raises we could give people and changing the review cycle to every six months rather than the usual annual review. We had hired Dan about two years earlier, right out of college. And the one hole in the company's pay raise policy was that it didn't deal with the tremendous increase in value between a newly hired programmer trainee and a good programmer with two years of solid experience.

In addition to understanding the market value of programmers, I had one other thing going for me. Since I worked for a small company, the only person I really had to convince that Dan was worth a twenty-five percent pay raise was Jim, our chief financial officer.

Fortunately I had a good relationship with Jim. I got my financials in on time and I followed the rules, two things that are important to chief financial officers. So when I came to him with this ridiculous request, I had a track record of being a sane and sensible manager. And since it was the right thing to do, Jim agreed to the raise. Of course, he insisted that the paperwork be done then and signed off on by the appropriate managers. And it wouldn't take effect until Dan's upcoming review date, a month or so away. Still, less than twenty-four hours after Dan first approached me, I was able to give him the paperwork for a matching offer, which he accepted.

Unfortunately, my task wasn't done yet. I realized that I had another programmer, Simeon, who had been hired as a programmer trainee about three months after Dan. He was another good programmer who was now significantly underpaid. Since I didn't want to come to Jim with the same request in three months, I asked for a raise for Simeon at the same time. Jim was a little tougher with this request. Since Simeon didn't have a job offer, we would phase in the large increase over two pay raise cycles. Both Simeon and I could live with that plan. He was even pleasantly surprised.

That was when Kelly made his comment that turned it into an imaginary trophy. I should also report that more than one person asked me "What do you have on Jim?"

The second imaginary trophy I acquired was on the marketing side of my job. We were trying to sell a systems development project to Xerox. I had been involved in producing the Functional Specification. So the Xerox people knew me and more importantly I knew them. They had an impossibly short timeframe for developing their system. I asked the VP in charge of the project the reason for the deadline and his answer made sense. Something about a projected paper shortage, I think. It wasn't just an arbitrary date when they thought the project should be done. Their in-house development staff had a proposal on the table that made the date. We couldn't do it. I wasn't convinced that their in-house people could either, but that was irrelevant.

I worked with other Rand managers to make the schedule as short as possible and it was still two months too long, I think it was eighteen months vs. the "required" sixteen months. Our salesman was unhappy that we couldn't do better because in-house development groups were always strong competition. I made the schedule presentation explaining why we thought our schedule reflected the shortest amount of time required for us to do our part of the project. I also underscored the risk our company was willing to take based on my evaluation of the high quality of the Xerox staff assigned to the project. We got the contract much to the amazement of our salesman. The VP in charge of the project was pleased that we wouldn't change our timeframe to match our competition even if it cost us the contract. It gave him confidence that our proposed schedule was doable. That's what made it one of my imaginary trophies.

***

One unexpected benefit of the Xerox project was that I was introduced to cross-country skiing. On one of the project trips, the Rand team ended up spending a weekend in January in Rochester, New York, where Xerox was headquartered. At first I considered it a case of bad planning on my part as there is a lot of snow and cold in Rochester in January. But the Xerox project manager suggested that we go cross-country skiing. Initially this seemed like a strange idea as there are no hills, much less mountains, in that area of upstate New York. It turned out that they transformed the golf courses around Rochester into cross-country skiing areas. The Xerox team managed to outfit all of the Rand team with appropriate clothes and skis and off we went. It was great fun. I had tried downhill skiing but it seemed like I was either going too fast or getting back on my feet after falling. Neither of these activities was much fun. But I loved cross-country skiing. It was like a walk in the woods at a time of the year that you don't normally go for a walk in the woods. I came home hooked on the sport and quickly acquired my own set of skis.

Me, John, Mom and Dad on cross-country skis

The cabin started getting more use as a result of my new sport as there was a good cross-country ski area, Bear Valley, up Hwy 4 from the cabin. The rest of the family was also becoming interested in cross-country skiing, and John and Candice came up to the cabin to ski several times. Unfortunately cross-country skiing became another activity Tony and I didn't share. He did continue to go up to the cabin on the trip that included New Year's Eve but that became his only winter trip to the cabin. Our separate lives continued as Tony stayed home to take care of the dogs while I was skiing.

***

Xerox turned out to be a shining star of a project. Based on advice from one of our VPs, I picked my most technically competent project manager, Dave F, to run the project. And he did a great job, bringing it in on the schedule we'd proposed.

But my other big project that kicked off at the same time was a disaster. I'm not sure that even having managed two large projects, Sun and Abbott, that I could have successfully managed this one. It was a big, functionally complex project with a difficult client. Jeff, the project manager I gave the job to, wasn't up to the job. If Ed had still been the department manager, I'm sure he could have helped Jeff, but I didn't know how. Eventually it got so bad we were in full bailout mode and I was running the project. But it was a mess and made Abbott look like a resounding success. We finally came up with a way for us to exit the project without destroying our company, but the system we delivered was a long way from functional.

A competent department manager would have spotted the problems with the project early, helped the project manager fix the things that were wrong and consulted with senior management before the project was in crisis mode. I had done none of those things.

I had been at Rand for ten years but I knew it was time to find another job. I wanted a job I could do and enjoy. Being a department manager was not that job. And Rand, as a small company, couldn't afford to keep staff that wasn't doing their job.

In spite of a sputtering economy, I found a job at Charles Schwab, Inc. quickly. They were looking for a project manager and I was confident about my skills in that type of a job.

Charles Schwab, Inc.

I STARTED WORK at Schwab the summer of 1983. It was the first time I had been hired as a manager, not as an individual contributor. Still, a job as project manager in the Special Projects area seemed to play to my strengths. Looking back at the projects I worked on, they are somewhat hard to believe today in the era of the internet. But this was the 1980s. Networks were rare except in very large companies and the IBM PC had just been developed. Technologically it was a different world. But the financial industry was at the forefront of using the latest technology.

My first project was called "Schwab Quotes." It needed a plan and I put one together. The project was to develop a program that would dial a printer plugged into a phone line at a scheduled time during the day and print out current quotes for a stock portfolio. In some ways the best part of the project was that I had one of these printers in my home and it was useful, or maybe just fascinating, to be able to easily get daily quotes of our stocks. The reason that I had stocks to follow is that Schwab had a 401K plan for employees. The nature of the 401K plan made it possible for the first time since I'd been married to take money out of my paycheck and save it. The fact that it was tax deductible and had an employer match was also good. I didn't know much about the stock market when I went to work at Schwab but it was a good place to learn.

Another interesting project was our backup Order Entry System. Schwab had a private network that linked its branches around the country to a central computer. People would call their branch to place an order to buy or sell securities, stocks, bonds or mutual funds, or get a quote. The branch would use their link to the central computer to complete the task. The ability to do this in those days was unusual.

The problem the backup system was designed to solve was a loss of connectivity. Periodically the link to the central computer could go down. This was usually caused by a network problem, but sometimes it was the central system itself that failed. This meant the branches had to take orders by hand and then enter them into the system after it came back up. This was extra work for the branches and when they were busy, this extra work could cause delays. We developed a backup system using one of the new IBM PCs in each branch. Instead of handwriting the order, it could be entered into the PC and when the connection to the central computer was restored, the PC could call the central computer and upload the orders. It was slick for those pre-World Wide Web days. Implementation was the tricky part of the project. We made the installation instructions for the branches as simple as possible. Still, there were problems. Any time you are installing new hardware and software in almost a hundred different locations something is bound to go wrong somewhere. Fortunately, all of the problems were solved with phone calls.

On some projects I worked on at Schwab it made sense to visit branch offices to see how things worked in the field. Whenever I would call to schedule a visit, the branch manager had a standard question.

"Are you registered so we can put you to work if we get busy?"

Being registered, or being a "registered rep" as it was sometimes referred to, meant that you had a National Association of Securities Dealers (NASD) license that allowed you to trade stocks and bonds. Mostly because I was tired of answering "no" to that question, I decided to sign up to get my NASD Series 7 license, the basic starting license for securities dealers.

One of the benefits of working for Schwab was that they encouraged all their employees to become registered and paid all of the costs of the training, the test and the license fee. Getting my license, however, had an amazing side effect. I chose the approach of a multi-day immersion class followed immediately by taking the licensing test. I passed without any problem. I left the office before taking the class confused, as usual, by what the business people were talking about. I returned to work after passing the test and, for the first time, I understood everything they were saying. I had acquired a whole new language. And it made a remarkable change in my understanding of the business of being a stockbroker.

***

For the first time in my management career I had female peers. Even before leaving Rand, I had been told that the financial industry had been a leader in moving women into management. One of the trips I made as department manager was to Jacksonville, Florida. A company headquartered there had expressed interest in Rand's basic system that we customized for each of our customers. Since they didn't need an Order Entry System for product sales, it wasn't clear that our system could be used for their needs. I was visiting to see if I could come up with an idea for something we could do for them. When they met me at the airport I made a comment about being easy to spot as there weren't too many businesswomen on the flight. One of the men I was meeting said they weren't surprised that Rand had sent a woman manager, as much of the work they did was in support of the financial industry and there were many women managers in that industry. It certainly turned out to be true at Schwab.

I remember one conversation particularly. I was talking to three coworkers, Geri, Charlotte and Dawn. In the middle of the conversation Geri made an thought provoking comment.

"Looking at the four of us, you would think that women have made lots of progress in having careers."

"Of course, we've made great progress." Dawn said.

"Not really." Geri responded. "I'm the only one with a child. Not having children is still a price most women pay for having a career."

I don't know how Geri had managed to be a single mother with a career. Had she been talking about a part of the system she was managing, I would have asked a follow-up question. But somehow it never occurred to me to ask probing questions about people's careers or their personal life.

Other women paid different prices for their career. Helen, who had been the only woman senior to me at the Sixth Army, was unmarried in her early forties when I knew her. But shortly before I left, she finally married. Two other successful women I worked with, Kaye, at Rand, and Janet, in a future job, both married for the first time in their early forties.

Times were changing though. Dawn, who wasn't married at the time of the conversation with Geri, married several years later and her husband, who had also had a technical management career at Schwab, stayed home to be the primary caregiver of their daughter after she was born.

***

Then, once again, I was promoted into the wrong job. This time I was not interested in the new job, but we were being reorganized and my old job was going away, and this was the only senior job available. This job was being creat-ed because the process of installing changes to Schwab's computer programs was haphazard and resulted in system failures more often than anyone was happy with.

The Computer Operations and System Development groups were constantly fighting. Was the systems failure the result of a programming error? Or was it caused by an op-erational miscue? Since both types of mistakes happened, it was easy for both groups to blame the other for the problem.

A new group was being created called Systems Management and its job was to develop and manage the process of making changes to Schwab's computer programs. To make the job of managing this group more politically challenging, the computer security function was added to the group's functions.

The reason the head of the IT department thought I was the right person for the job was my varied background. I understood the different types of changes that had to be made and, to some extent, what their constraints were. But he either misunderstood the nature of the job or my skills. It wasn't a technical job and my technical skills that he thought would be so important to the job were really more "nice to have" skills, not critical ones. Being the operational manager of an emotionally charged process required people skills I didn't have.

Initially, I did okay. After all, the first thing that needed to be done was to develop a process to manage change and I was a development person. But running a control function played to none of my strengths. And even worse, it activated many of my weaknesses. My goal became to figure out how to get out of this job before my inability to do it well was obvious.

There was one advantage to having a job I was ill-suited for. Working extra hours didn't accomplish any more than working regular hours did. So I had time for family events and outdoor activities.

Family Reunion

W̲E HELD OUR first family reunion in July 1982 at Ft. Worden in Port Townsend, Washington. Mom was inspired to organize a reunion for the families of Dad and his two brothers after Dad's sister-in-law, Aunt Regi, died at sixty-two.

The family now consisted of three generations. It had grown from three brothers to almost forty people. There were twenty-seven of us at the reunion. The five surviving members of the oldest generation, Mom, Dad, Uncle Carl, Uncle Paul and his wife, Aunt Charlotte, were all there. Nine of the thirteen cousins, my generation, made it. Dad was well represented as his entire family was there. Mom and Dad picked up the cost of staying at Ft. Worden for all of us. Dad had retired from the navy in 1972 and gone to work as an engineer for a private firm. So for the first time in their married life they had money. In addition to Tony and me, John was there with his wife, Candice, and her daughter Beth. Pat and Tom showed up with their son Rob. Pat was pregnant with Reed who was to arrive in December. The three unmarried siblings, Maggie, Dan and Chris came by themselves. Uncle Paul's whole family consisting of Paul Jr., his wife Lanette and their daughter Sarah; and Don, his wife Ann and their two children, Bruce and Erica, were there as well. In addition to Uncle Carl, only his daughter Kate, her husband Hank and their two daughters, Desiree and Juliet, made it to the reunion. Paul Jr. and Lanette's daughter Sarah was fifteen and the oldest of the third generation. Pat and Tom's son Rob, who was three, was the youngest.

Ft. Worden was an old army base. Construction began on the fort in 1897 and it was activated as an army base in 1902. It became a Washington State Park in 1973. The movie *An Officer and a Gentleman* was filmed at Ft. Worden. We stayed in a group of houses that had been officers' quarters when the fort was an active army base. The houses were actually duplexes and the duplexes ranged in size from three bedrooms with one-and-a-half baths to six bedrooms and three-and-a-half baths. Each duplex had a large kitchen, dining room and living room. These created lots of room for the large family group to gather in.

There was plenty to do in the area. The parade grounds in front of the house were a great area for impromptu football games. Port Townsend had become a touristy town and the shops on the main street were fun to walk through. We went hiking on Hurricane Ridge in nearby Olympic National Park and took the ferry to Victoria on Vancouver Island in Canada. Pictures were taken at a photo shop that had old-time clothes you could dress up in. A memorable event of the Victoria visit was high tea at the Empress Hotel.

Mom made a booklet for everyone. It contained a number of family pictures. The oldest picture included was of Grandpa as a small boy. A family tree for each of the three brothers was also in the booklet. These family trees have been useful over the years in figuring out how old everyone is. The booklet also contained the only known picture that shows Paul, Jr. being taller than his younger brother Don.

We were to have four more family reunions at Ft. Worden, in 1992, 1997, 2000 and 2005. The first one, however, was special as it was the only reunion with all three of the brothers in attendance. Uncle Carl died the following year, 1983, on my birthday. Both Maggie and I went back to Chicago for his funeral. There we saw Kate and Hank again and the four cousins, Mike, Liz, Jim and Tom, and the three spouses, Bill, Jane and Tona, who had not made it to the Ft. Worden reunion. Mike was there by himself. Maggie thinks he may have still been married to Judy, his second wife, but she and their son Nick didn't come to the funeral. Mike's son from his first marriage, Mike Jr., didn't make it either. Liz and Bill's two girls, Lisha and Regi, were also there.

Unlike with earlier family deaths, I actively grieved for Uncle Carl. I had gotten to know him well during my college years. I had seen him earlier that year as I'd stopped by for a visit on a business trip. Dad also grieved for Uncle Carl. They had always been close. It was the first time I remember Dad grieving. He was very subdued and talked a lot about how close they had been. When my brother John died at sixty-seven, slightly older than Uncle Carl had been when he died, I experienced firsthand the grief of losing a sibling and that it felt so much more intense than losing a parent.

One of the reasons I may have grieved for Uncle Carl was that I was getting over the idea that "people are only in my life temporarily." Part of it was that I had been living in the same place, the San Francisco Bay Area, for fourteen years by then. But as an adult I had much more control over who I kept in touch with. I was still in contact with friends from Maryknoll High School, Marquette University and from my last three jobs, FDIC, the Sixth Army and Rand.

Later in the summer of 1983, we had a partial family reunion of our branch of the family. Maggie was on the west coast for a wedding in Tacoma, Washington. Then she went with friends on a trip to Hawaii so a stop in San Francisco on her way home to Philadelphia made sense. She brought leis with her from Hawaii. Mom and Dad were planning on coming to San Francisco to spend time with their new grandson Reed who had been born in December 1982. John, Candice and Beth came up from southern California to make it even more of a family event. By then Don, Ann, Bruce and Erica were living in Mountain View, California, and they came over for an extended family dinner.

Most of the family in July 1983 in our front yard. In back: Tom, holding Reed, Pat, holding Rob, Candice, Dad, Mom and Tony. In front: Maggie, Beth, John, Dante, me and Diablo. Dan and Chris are missing from the picture. They didn't make the trip to California.

There was one more family death in 1983. Gram died on John's birthday. She was eighty-eight. I went to Bremerton for the funeral. Tony stayed home to take care of the dogs. Gram's short-term memory had been deteriorating for years but she always knew who we were. In talking to her you would have the same conversation over and over again because of the memory loss. Everyone had a different conversation with her. Mom tried to keep Gram at home until the end but finally a few months before she died, Mom and Dad had to move her to a nursing home. I didn't grieve as much for Gram as I had for Uncle Carl. Her death was not unexpected and at eighty-eight it seemed like she had lived a full life. And with her memory problems, she may have been ready to go.

The family continued to grow as Chris married Marian in 1984 and Dan married Zina in 1987.

I reached the "advanced" age of forty and that remains the only milestone birthday that I don't remember. It must not have been a big deal. It may have been one of the advantages of being married to an older man as I remained much younger than he was. By then Tony was fifty-six. The other marker of the passage of time was an invitation to the twenty-fifth anniversary of my high school graduation the spring before my forty-third birthday. I had always planned to attend that reunion but instead of holding it in Honolulu where I had graduated, the class decided to hold it in Las Vegas. I suppose it was an excuse for classmates, who had remained in Hawaii, to get away from the island for a while, but for me it was a big disappointment and I didn't go.

The social change that impacted me the most was discovering that gays and lesbians were part of my life. Harvey Milk, the first openly gay San Francisco supervisor, had been assassinated in 1978 when I was thirty-four. Because of his work and that of others, people were starting to come out of the closet. I acquired a good friend who happened to be a lesbian. I wasn't sure about the proposed domestic partnership law but I remember telling someone that "it would be a good thing for Sukey and Natalie." Knowing people with a different sexual orientation changes your perspective. Things like domestic partnerships and later gay marriage weren't just abstract topics for discussion. They impacted people you knew and liked.

Then the AIDS epidemic hit. I don't remember exactly when it started filling the Bay Area news but San Francisco bath houses were closed to help slow its spread in 1984, the year I turned forty. It wasn't just a news event. I knew people who were dying or had died. And I knew people who were losing close friends. With no treatment in sight, it was a scary time.

Dogs and Volksmarches

OUR FIRST DOG Diablo died unexpectedly in April 1985. He was only ten. It was cancer, which we didn't even realize he had until it was so bad that the only choice available was to end his suffering. I was devastated and it was six months before I could talk about him without crying. Right after Diablo died, Tony said that the only thing to do was to get another dog immediately. We went to a different German Shepherd breeder this time and seven-week-old Bravo joined the pack in May 1985. Dante who was nine and a half was not at all pleased with the new addition, but she warmed up to him. The other "person" who missed Diablo was Skipper, the sheltie who lived next door. Skipper had first come to visit as a small, fit-in-the-palm-of-your-hand puppy and he and Diablo became best friends. The problem was that with Diablo gone, Skipper thought he was now the head dog in the house and started marking his territory inside our house. His visits quickly stopped.

Bravo's first visit to the cabin was interesting. Dante's hip dysplasia was getting worse and she was not allowed to roam outside but was quickly moved from the car into the house as was Bravo, who was just a puppy. We had never had a problem with raccoons at the cabin because the scent of dogs kept them away. But with both dogs in the house and not allowed to roam outside there was no warning scent and the first night we were at the cabin, raccoons appeared on our deck. We put Dante on a leash and opened the door a bit. She barked; the raccoons left and never came back.

I also started taking Bravo on Volksmarches. Maggie introduced me to this type of organized walking. She had discovered Volksmarching when she lived in Germany, where the sport originated. American military personnel stationed in Europe had brought Volksmarches back to the United States and the sport quickly spread across the country. The basic concept was that you completed a designated ten-kilometer walk and at the end received an award. I liked walking, and getting an award for doing it seemed like icing on the cake. Awards were usually pins or patches that commemorated the particular walk. Bravo was perfectly capable of doing the ten kilometers, roughly six miles, that the walk entailed. I always registered him so he received his own award at the end.

One of the Volksmarches that we did was sponsored by the President's Fitness Council. They apparently sold some of the names and addresses of those who did the walk because Bravo got on a mailing list and for years there were advertisements in our mail addressed to him. John and Candice also got interested in Volksmarching. They and their cocker spaniel Pearl joined Maggie, Bravo and me on a Volksmarch in Grass Valley, California. We would later do Volksmarches with them in the Seattle area without dogs.

Maggie had moved to San Francisco in May 1984. Unlike when Pat and I moved to San Francisco, she had a job offer before she moved. With her arrival, all four of the oldest siblings were living in California. John was living near Santa Barbara. Only Dan and Chris remained Washingtonians near Mom and Dad. This was to change as Pat and family moved to Seattle in June 1986. John and family also moved to Seattle in 1988. In both cases the moves were caused by the need to find a new job. Maggie, however, stayed in California and in December 1986 she bought a home in Albany, just north of Berkeley. At first Dad was reluctant to help her buy the house. Unlike Pat and me, she wasn't married. Fortunately, he came to his senses. His attitude was a little unusual even then and today, in retrospect, it seems bizarre. However, it is staggering to remember that women were not guaranteed equal access to credit in their own name until the Equal Credit Opportunity Act was passed in 1974.

In March 1988, Dante's hip dysplasia finally got so bad that we had to put her down. She was twelve and looked very old. It was hard to decide when to let her go as her deterioration had been so long and so steady. It took the night she whimpered most of the night to make the decision. We probably waited too long as she had obviously been in pain for a while.

Bravo needed a companion so we got another girl dog that I named Chelsea. Tony decided that since he had named the first three dogs, it was my turn. She was the first dog we ever had that got carsick but she wasn't the last. Unlike our first two dogs, Diablo and Dante, Bravo and Chelsea were not related but they got along fine from the beginning. As with Dante, the breeder wanted a litter from Chelsea. Tony hadn't changed his mind about not neutering male dogs so we had some rough times keeping our two dogs apart before the breeders were ready to have Chelsea come up to be bred. After two failed attempts we said no more. Fortunately they agreed and we were able to spay Chelsea. She was a beautiful dog and probably would have had beautiful puppies but this outcome was clearly the best one for us. In spite of all of our problems, Tony and I kept caring for the dogs as something important to both of us.

I wasn't happy with my marriage in my mid-forties and thoughts of divorce were more frequent. Tony and I were doing almost nothing together and his heavy drinking continued. But my life had some stability to it. I wasn't up to the disruption a divorce would create in my life. We might have to sell the house and then what would happen to the dogs? The dogs were part of my stability. Mom always referred to them as "your kids." I knew they weren't but it gave me a place to direct whatever maternal instincts I had.

Chelsea and Bravo

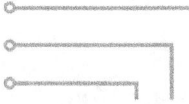

New Zealand

THE IDEA OF a ski trip to New Zealand started the summer of 1987 when Maggie and I were bemoaning the fact that ski season was still months away. She and I had been using our cabin a lot as we were both cross-country skiing.

Then one of us said, "If we were in New Zealand now, we could be skiing."

It was something to look forward to in the heat of a California summer.

By the spring of 1988 when we needed to start planning for real, she let me know that there was no way she could make the trip. Maggie's job had been moved to New Jersey in July 1987 and she didn't want to move back to the east coast. By the following spring she hadn't found a new job. She had been making do with temporary jobs. By late 1988 she would have steady work as an independent contractor, but she didn't know that when she backed out of the trip.

I was really glad when Dad offered to go with me. Between being in the wrong job and having a failed marriage, I desperately needed a vacation to recharge my batteries and improve my outlook on life. Since retiring, Dad had been active. This wasn't going to be his first cross-country ski trip; he had gone with a group to Yellowstone the previous winter. In addition, he was part of the local mountain rescue group and had climbed Mount Rainier twice. He was definitely the more fit of the two of us even though he was twenty-five years older than I was. We celebrated his sixty-ninth birthday on the trip.

It had been twenty-six years since our previous trip together when we went to Japan after I graduated from high school. On that trip he was very much in charge. On this trip it was almost a trip of equals. I say "almost" as Dad always remained my father, not my friend.

Because of all of the business travel I had been doing, I had plenty of airline miles and bought us business class tickets to Auckland. Dad picked up the cost of all of our travel in New Zealand. We split all of the other expenses between us and because we tended to think alike, we had no problems agreeing on our travel plans. We planned an epic trip. We would be helicoptered up Mount Cook and would ski down the glacier. It would take several days with overnight stops at huts on the glacier. Then we would do a little sightseeing in New Zealand.

We met at the Los Angeles International airport to board our transpacific flight. Dad had begun his journey at the

Seattle airport and I had started from the San Francisco airport. Uncle Paul, who lived in nearby Long Beach, came to the Los Angeles airport to see us off.

We arrived in Auckland, after a refueling stop in Honolulu, in early August 1988. It was my first trip south of the equator, and Dad let me know that making my first crossing in an airplane could not compare with the traditions associated with crossing the equator for the first time on shipboard. I was happy with just a certificate that recorded my "accomplishment." Since we arrived in Auckland early in the morning, we had most of the day to explore the city. It was winter in New Zealand but because Auckland was on the north island the weather was mild, similar to southern California in the winter. That night I had my first meal of New Zealand lamb. The waiter told us that they exported the best lamb to other countries and that what we were eating was not their best. That was hard to believe as it was the best lamb I'd ever eaten.

Early the next morning we boarded a flight to Mount Cook on the south island. The resort area, at 2500 feet, was below the snowline. After checking into our hotel we stopped by the office of Alpine Guides and met our guide for our ski trip down the glacier. In spite of a dry winter, there was apparently enough snow up the mountain that we would be able to ski without problem. However, they did report that there was a forecast of fog for the next day. If that forecast proved to be correct, we might not be able to start our trip on schedule as the helicopter would not be able to fly us up the mountain to our starting point. Hoping for the best, we went on a hike up one of the nearby hills. It was a strenuous hike as the trail we took was a steep one. It was the first time I had ever hiked a trail where steps had been added to help control erosion. Two impressions linger from that afternoon and evening. The first was that most of our fellow tourists were Japanese. The second was the lack of wool souvenir clothing. With sheep being such a big industry in New Zealand, I was expecting lots of wool sweaters to be available at the resort gift shops. Most of what they had was cotton.

The weather forecast of fog turned out to be correct. Our guide suggested that we just postpone the trip a day and go skiing at a nearby downhill ski resort. So that's what we did. We weren't the only cross-country skiers at the ski area but we were definitely outnumbered by the downhill skiers. It was nice to be able to tune up our skiing legs before starting out on the mountain. Additionally it was fun to spend time with a New Zealander and to allow him to show off his country. There were the usual differences in the English language to be dealt with. For example, New Zealanders don't have ranches; they have farms for both plants and animals. And they domesticate deer, so there were deer farms as well as sheep farms. Venison was not uncommon on menus.

Unfortunately the weather on the mountain hadn't improved by the next day, and there was no guarantee that the weather would be good enough for a helicopter flight even the following day. After much discussion, Dad and I decided to do a tour of the country instead. Alpine Guides was willing to give us back much of our prepaid tour money. We laid out a new itinerary and caught a flight south to Queenstown that afternoon.

The next day we took a jeep tour of Skipper Canyon on the Shotover River. The warning sign at the start of the road through the canyon said "Extreme Care Necessary," but we were in a four-wheel drive vehicle with an experienced driver so it didn't seem too bad. Some of the tours were by motor coach and they looked a little more dangerous. It was a small tour, just our driver, Dad, me and a couple from Australia. There was good-natured banter between the New Zealand driver and the Australian couple about the relative merits of the citizens of the two countries. However, it was obvious they shared a language they all could understand, as periodically I had to ask for a translation. Part of my difficulties came from slang words and part of it was just accent. The description of the tour listed it as covering both scenery and history. The river canyon was indeed awesome. And it was gold mining country so there were old bridges, houses and cemeteries to look at as well as gold mining equipment.

We then took a bus to Dunedin on the east coast of the south island. Halfway through the drive we met the bus coming from Dunedin and the drivers switched buses. That way both of them could return to their homes at the end of the day. Dunedin was laid out by the Free Church of Scotland to resemble Edinburgh. Many of the streets in the two cities share names. The time in Dunedin was the first gloomy weather we'd had on the trip. But we had fun visiting the

Early Otago Settlers Museum, Olveston and Lanarch Castle. The museum reinforced the knowledge that we had started to pick up in Auckland about how young of a "European" country New Zealand was. By New Zealand standards, the United States is an old country.

After leaving Dunedin we took the train up the east coast of New Zealand to Christchurch. We were almost back to our original travel plan but we arrived in Christchurch two days ahead of the original schedule and we needed a hotel for two nights. We could have gone to the hotel the travel agent had booked for us, but decided to stay near the train station. Unlike in many United States cities at the time, the neighborhoods around train stations in New Zealand were good areas of town. It was another moment that left me thinking that New Zealand was like I imagined the United States being in the 1950s, a quieter, less violent time.

Dad left me at the train station with all of our luggage and skis, that we had had to lug all over New Zealand with us, and went in search of a hotel. The proprietor of the hotel drove him back to the train station so we wouldn't have to carry everything to the hotel. We finally did some shopping in Christchurch and I got the wool sweater I had wanted as a souvenir. On one of the tours, Dad struck up a conversation with an older English couple. It turned out that both the husband and wife were sixty-eight. They told Dad that this was probably their last trip abroad; they were getting too old for traveling. Dad didn't tell them that he had turned sixty-nine on the trip and was actually older than they were. He looked a lot younger.

My favorite stop in Christchurch was the Hall of Antarctic Discovery in the Canterbury Museum. That exhibit contained clothing and supplies from early expeditions to Antarctica as many of them departed from Christchurch. The most surprising thing was the china, actual china, used by one of the early expeditions. But of course they had none of the camping supplies that have been invented over the intervening years. On our last day in Christchurch we moved to our originally planned Christchurch hotel near the airport. We were back on the original schedule and about to fly to Rotorua on the north island. Rotorua rounded out our New Zealand experience with volcanic hot springs, a visit to a zoo and watching sheep shearing. We also attended some Maori cultural events. Then we returned to Auckland. By changing our trip from a skiing vacation to a tour of the country, we had managed to see much more of the country than originally planned. I have no regrets about our choice. We also had time for one more activity in Auckland before returning home. We went for a catamaran cruise on Auckland bay.

It had been a nice trip. Dad and I were comfortable together as we enjoyed doing the same things. In retrospect, it seems surprising that I didn't seek Dad's advice on my job problems. After all he had had two successful careers, first in the navy and then as a civilian engineer. But we had never really talked about my career. And because I was trying to forget about the job for a while, it didn't seem like the time to start that conversation.

On the way home from New Zealand, I flew to Seattle with Dad because Paul Jr.'s daughter Sarah was getting married the weekend we came home. Sarah's wedding had an unexpected benefit. All thirteen cousins were in town. Paul Jr., as the father of the bride, arranged to have the wedding photographer take a group picture of all thirteen cousins. He then ordered copies and sent one to each of us. It was a nice thing for him to do. The last time all of the cousins had been together was in 1951 and there had only been nine of us then.

Then the trip was over and I had to go back to work at a job I hated. I resolved to find a new job and started going on job interviews. But I wasn't getting any job offers. I wasn't totally failing as a candidate because I did get invited back for additional interviews for some of the jobs I applied for. At least once I was told I came in second for the position. On the other hand there was one job I was feeling good about. Then I had an interview with the manager of the business area I would be supporting if I got the job. The interview felt awkward. But I was unprepared when they told me why I was no longer in the running for the job. The manager's assessment was that I had "absolutely no management skills." I hoped he was wrong as I needed to have the salary of a management job in order to make enough money to manage our pile of debts.

Fifteen years earlier, when I had faced problems with both my marriage and my job, I had found balance in my life by fixing the job situation. That approach wasn't working this time. Something had to change. Again I got lucky. Although at the time it didn't seem like good luck.

"A Canter is the Cure for All Evils"

- Benjamin Disraeli

Beginnings and an End

BY THE TIME of the New Zealand trip, I had firmly established cross-country skiing as my winter sport and realized I needed a summer sport. Like cross-country skiing, my summer sport had to be something that could be done without an opponent or a team. It also needed to be something done outside. Dennis, a coworker first at Rand and then at Schwab, had been inspired by the movie *The Man from Snowy River* to try horseback riding. He seemed to be enjoying it so I decided to give it a try. I had been on a horse a number of times before then but it wasn't something I was thrilled with. I had no idea how horses were about to take over my life.

For my forty-fifth birthday Tony gave me a present of as many riding lessons as I wanted. I had my first lesson on June 17, 1989. This wasn't a memorable date that stuck in my mind but since that June I also started keeping a journal I could look up the date. Journaling started because Mom and Dad gave me *A Book of Days*. Pages on one side of the book had pictures from Monet at Giverny; the pages on the other side had space to write about the day. On post-it notes inside the front cover, Mom had written "They say everyone has the material for at least one book—here you go dear. Write the nice things that happen each day—or just how you feel— Happy B'day. Love Mom & Dad."

My second entry in the new journal, on June 9, says "It looks like it is going to be an interesting year. Today I was effectively told I will be laid off in five weeks. The overriding emotion seems to be—ok that's over let's get on with the next job—finding a new job. There's some residual anger and it's embarrassing to tell anyone. So far Tony is the only one I've told."

Although I was hurt, embarrassed and angry to be laid off, I wasn't surprised. I was in the wrong job and couldn't get out of it. I might have been successful in finding another job at Schwab if the Senior Vice President (SVP) in charge of Information Technology (IT), who had hired me, had not left Schwab. The only history I had with the IT SVP who replaced him was that I was doing a bad job. And I was doing it so badly that when the new SVP reorganized the IT group, no one wanted me on their staff. A job was created for me. Several months later, the job was eliminated as unnecessary, which it was, and I was fired. Well, technically, I wasn't fired; I was laid off because my job had been eliminated.

It is hard to think of being fired as a good thing, but, in this case, it was. The last ten years had beaten the spunky kid who announced that someday she was "going to the moon" into submission. The ambitious teenager who skillfully navigated the career path from scientist to medical doctor to computer programmer had lost her way. I had let others define the environment in which I had to live. The very thing I had struggled against as a younger person. And the worst thing was that I had no idea that was what I was doing. My goal of being the best me I could be had been sidetracked into trying to do my best at a job I wasn't at all suited to. So when Schwab said to me, in essence, "Go figure out what you are doing with the rest of your life someplace else," I had no choice but to finally pay attention. I could no longer be distracted by trying to do the job I was so terrible at.

The fact that I had started riding lessons was a lifesaver. The lessons gave me something new to do and something interesting to learn while I was struggling with the horrible prospect of finding a new job.

Fortunately Schwab gave me a safety net when they let me go. They gave me almost five months of severance pay through the end of 1989. And because I was a senior person and Schwab was a large company, they provided me with an outplacement service whose function was to help me find a new job. I had a counselor at the outplacement service who kept me focused about finding a new job. One of the first things in that process was to take a series of tests. These tests were designed to help them figure out what type of person

I was and thus help them steer me towards a job that suited my talents. One of the tests was the Myers Briggs Personality Assessment. I was classified as an INTP: Introverted Intuitive Thinking Perceiving.

In their book *Type Talk*, Otto Kroeger and Janet M. Thuesen begin their description of an INTP with, "If any type personifies the absentminded professor, it would likely be the INTP." When you looked at it that way, it wasn't surprising that I, the "absentminded professor," had trouble with a job that had lots of time-sensitive details needing to be sorted out while dealing with unhappy people. I recognized all the traits that my Myers Briggs type was identified with. It gave me a new way of thinking about how I liked to work. But the most useful thing I learned from Myers Briggs was how different people were. For example, I always had trouble understanding people when they weren't being "rational." That was the "T" in my Myers Briggs type—a Thinker. Now, using my new knowledge I could realize that they weren't being difficult; they were just being true to their type. Also I learned that Myers Briggs defined an introvert, the "I" in my type, as a person who uses energy when interacting with people. No wonder being a manager wore me out. In order to do my job properly, I estimated I had to spend seventy-five percent of my time working with people.

The Myers Briggs information didn't really help me with my job search. But in the future it would help me adjust my approach to allow me to interact better with coworkers. It wasn't until much later that I would use it to better understand friends and family.

Some people in the outplacement service found jobs quickly. Others took a long time. I fell somewhere in the middle. If I could have just looked for a job as a programmer or a systems designer, I could have found a job quickly. But we were in a financial mess with our large debts, and I was having enough trouble managing our bills with a management level salary. So I had to look for a management job.

The trouble with looking for a management job was that I really didn't want one. For almost twenty years, I had been in and out of management jobs and for the most part I was more productive and happier when I wasn't a manager. The reason was simple. On a scale of one to ten, I was a five or a six as a manager. Occasionally I would have moments of brilliance and be a seven or an eight. On the other hand I was consistently a seven or an eight as an individual contributor and in moments of brilliance I could be a nine or a ten.

Then I got lucky again. A woman, Vernel, whom I had met in the outplacement service, was hired as the head of a small IT department for an insurance company. As she started her new job, she decided to establish some procedures for the department. She offered me a job as a consultant to develop some change management procedures. The hourly rate she was willing to pay was enough that I could manage our bills on it. It was a short-term job, only a couple of months, but that gave me two more months to find a job, so I took it. This job had a benefit other than money. As I started analyzing how Vernel's department worked, I was reminded that I wasn't the failure I had been at Schwab. I was capable of doing good work. It was the shot in the arm I needed to keep my job search going.

I received other help as well. One surprising source of help came from two men who had worked for me. Bruce had been an employee at Rand and Clive had been a contractor at Schwab. I have no idea why these men decided to make finding me a job an important task for them, but they did. They fed me leads on jobs, acted as references and even helped set up interviews. I didn't know either of them well before my job search and after I found a job they went back to being just people I knew slightly.

However, my next job came from an unexpected place. Ed, my old boss from Rand, had started a small consulting company with another former Rand employee, John F. They had a contract with an oil company in Taiwan to develop a Functional Specification for an Order Entry System and needed a third person. I wasn't interested at first. Doing analysis in a foreign language was difficult and I wasn't thrilled with the idea of being away from home for ten weeks.

I worried that, because of his heavy drinking, Tony would be incapable of managing our finances and I would come home to a house without utilities or in foreclosure. And on a more emotional level, my concern was that he wouldn't be able to take care of the dogs. Chelsea was barely a year old, still basically a puppy. Tony's drinking had made him more isolated but he still had contact with a few old friends and hopefully they would provide him support while I was gone. He thought I was being a worrywart and it did occur to me that having responsibility might be good for him.

There didn't seem to be any other jobs on the horizon and the pay for this one was good. Money would be automatically deposited in our bank account monthly. So I decided to take the job. The day after I accepted Ed and John's offer, Clive, the contractor who had worked for me at Schwab, told me of a contract at Visa that I would be perfect for. When I told him my plans he said to give him a call when I returned home. He was sure there would be another contract at Visa for me by then.

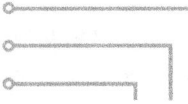

Taiwan

TAIWAN WAS MY **sixteenth country.** It was also the first country, other than the United States, that I had stayed in for any length of time. So I had time to go from being fascinated by a new country, to being frustrated because it was different, to finally learning to appreciate what made it unique.

I left for Taipei, Taiwan, on Thursday, March 1, 1990. Because of the International Date Line, it was late Friday before I arrived. The flight was not direct and I had to change airplanes in Tokyo. I spent Friday night in a hotel near the Taipei airport. I was exhausted from the long trip and the time zone change. All I managed to do on Saturday was move to my "permanent" hotel, the local YMCA. Outside of the United States, YMCAs were often used by business travelers for long-term lodging.

On Sunday I was feeling rested and took a tour of the National Museum. It contained large amounts of Chinese art that had been removed from the mainland when Chiang Kai-shek fled to Taiwan. I discovered I had arrived in a part of the world where I was illiterate. Everything was written in Chinese characters. When I was in Europe I could at least recognize words even if I didn't know what they meant. In Taiwan I had no idea what anything meant. I didn't remember this from my trip to Japan in 1962 but it was probably true there too.

I started work on Monday. The language problem was as bad as I was expecting. I didn't realize how much there was to be learned from reading material at the client site until I found myself unable read anything. Still, I was fascinated by Chinese characters and I started to recognize repeating characters. We weren't working directly for the Chinese oil company. Ed and John had a subcontract with IBM who was in charge of the whole project. IBM assigned a local employee, David, to help us. His help included assistance as I started trying to learn some Chinese.

Taipei was crowded and smoggy. Most people got around on motorbikes. I was impressed by the number of people that could be crammed onto a single bike. Initially I was bothered by the fact that it was so crowded you couldn't walk down the street without being bumped by another pedestrian. By the end of the trip I had gotten used to it. We ate a combination of Chinese and American food. The "Y" served American breakfasts, which was a good thing. We had our favorite restaurants including one that catered to Americans and sold "I survived Taiwan" t-shirts. I bought one before I left. We ate a lot of Chinese food, but as I told someone before I left on the trip, "I like Chinese food."

Getting paid for our expenses became a problem. It was a bureaucratic issue. I had a per diem contract with John and Ed so I knew I'd be okay in the end, but sometimes I was a little short on cash. Taiwan was a cash society. Occasionally you could use a credit card but it wasn't the norm. Frequently I was walking around with large amounts of cash in my pocket. That was a little unnerving.

I called home a few times. Tony called to report that the checks were showing up in the bank account, and I called Mom to wish her happy birthday in late April. Some of the calls were just to say hi. Times had really changed in the twenty years since my European trip where contact with someone overseas was all by mail.

Early in the stay I made a solo trip to the Taroko Gorge. It was a long, narrow gorge cut through hard stone, much of which was marble. I also visited the nearby marble factory. Guides conducted tours in Chinese, Japanese and English. I was the only native English speaker on the tour with the English-speaking guide. The others on the tour were from Europe. Later in the stay John, David and I took a long weekend and went to Alishan, the highest mountain on Taiwan.

The thing to do was to watch the sun rise over Alishan. So we were up at 4:30 a.m. trudging through the dark to the viewing spot. There were lots of other people making the trek. The most interesting part of that trip was the train trip up the mountain. As we climbed to higher elevations, we left the tropics and went through various climate zones to an area that looked similar to the California Sierra Nevada Mountains. Taiwan had cypress trees, not cedar trees, but other than that it was the same. Since this was late in the trip I felt we had to bring a present back to the rest of the team. David was no help in deciding what to bring as a gift. I decided on tea and we went tea tasting to decide what to get. Unfortunately John, David and I weren't good at tea tasting. The team was polite and drank our gift but it was obvious that the tea wasn't up to their normal standards.

Our final trip on Taiwan was to the north coast. We had our end-of-project lunch at a fabulous seafood restaurant. The Chinese members of the team went to the tanks of fish and picked out our meal. I have never had such good seafood. We were driven to the restaurant in a company van. The van driver joined us for lunch. The Chinese team members seemed surprised that I was surprised.

"After all," one of them told me, "he has to eat lunch too."

After lunch we went on a short cruise on a military boat. Because of the tense situation with the People's Republic of China, the coast of the island was constantly patrolled and no private boats were allowed in the water.

The Taiwan Project Team

During my stay in Taiwan, I also made a trip to Hong Kong. I was scheduled to be in Taiwan for ten weeks but my visa was only good for fifty days. There were two ways to handle this. The first was to go to a police station and get an extension of your visa. The second was to leave the country and return. When you returned your visa was automatically good for another fifty days. I chose option two. My flight to Hong Kong was early afternoon on a Friday so I went into the office in the morning. The Chinese team members were surprised to see me.

"You are going on an international flight," they said, "why are you here?"

I, on the other hand, just viewed it as a short hour-and-a-half flight so it was no big deal. When you live on a small island like Taiwan, your view of distance is different than when you live in the United States.

I quickly learned that in Hong Kong they spoke Cantonese Chinese. In Taiwan they spoke Mandarin Chinese. I didn't realize this at first as the characters were the same, but as soon as I tried to use the little Chinese I'd picked up in Taiwan, I realized that my language skills were useless in Hong Kong. But more people did speak English and pointing always worked.

It was nice to be someplace different and "downtown" Hong Kong was more European than Asian. I took a bus trip out to the border with the People's Republic of China and that area reminded me of Taiwan. I also used a tram to go up Victoria Peak, a noted tourist attraction, and ended the day with a dinner cruise on the bay. And of course I did some shopping. I tried to get into the spirit of negotiating every price but I wasn't good at it. My last purchase on the trip was a small bag to hold my purchases during the airplane trip back to Taipei. I'd only brought a small suitcase with me. When I realized that, at best, it was only going to be less than a dollar cheaper after I negotiated a price, I just paid the marked price. The man in the store looked disappointed, but I was tired.

On my last Sunday in Taipei, I realized I had only taken a few pictures of the city. So I took my camera and went out to take pictures. One of the places I visited was the Chiang Kai-shek Plaza. They were having a political demonstration for an upcoming election and many people were handing out political material. At first no one gave me anything; after all, it was obvious I wasn't from there. But then someone handed me a flyer and after that, everyone started handing me their papers. As I was standing there taking in the sights, I noticed a young Chinese man looking at me.

"Do you have any idea what is going on?" he asked in a perfect Midwestern accent.

I did, as the topic of politics had come up with the Chinese members of the team. I told him what I knew. Because he looked like he belonged there, he had more political handouts than I did.

I bought presents for people at home while I was in Taiwan and sent postcards to people who had requested one. I also bought a few presents for team members. David gave us each a set of three Chinese gods carved in wood. I can't remember what I gave him but know I gave him something because he had been a lifesaver more than once. Plus he did a good job of improving my knowledge of Chinese, both spoken and written.

There is a story behind why we got the Chinese gods. One dinner when David had joined us, he pointed out to us the Chinese god of money. Both John and I said we needed to get one of those to take home with us. Our searches were unsuccessful and so David got us the set of three gods. The other two gods were of happiness and health. I bought a pair of jade temple dragons to protect them. After all, I needed souvenirs too.

We produced an adequate Functional Specification and a preliminary database design. They were written in English. All of the Taiwanese members of the team read English. Their understanding of spoken English and their ability to converse in English varied widely.

The reason I say it was an adequate Functional Specification was that our knowledge of the system was bounded by what the Taiwanese team told us. We may have understood their system, but there was doubt in my mind that we did. Many times during a systems design process, I'd uncovered new information as a result of something I found in system documentation or by listening to a side conversation among client participants in the project. We had no access to written documentation because we were illiterate in Chinese and most of the conversations between the client team members were in Chinese.

One of the most frustrating afternoons in my career occurred in Taiwan.

In answer to what seemed like an innocuous question, two of the Taiwanese members of the team started arguing in Chinese. It quickly escalated to five or six people joining the argument. I asked the team member sitting next to me what was going on and he, uncharacteristically, brushed me off. When I repeated the question, he stood up and moved to another part of the room. I had been running the meeting, not an unusual occurrence, and it was clear that I had lost control of what was going on. Both Ed and John were off somewhere at the time so I couldn't discuss with them what to do. Ed checked later with the Taiwanese project manager and was assured that the topic being discussed had nothing to do with the design of the system. Still, when your job is to document the facts of how the system works, any disagreement usually provides some information, even if a discussion of the topic leads to a dead end.

I left for home before Ed and John, who were staying for another week or two to present our documents. But I was glad to be done and heading home. I left for home on May 12, and arrived on the same day. The International Date Line works in your favor coming home.

Tony had kept our finances in order while I was gone. The paperwork needed some cleaning up, but the bills had all been paid. My worries had been unfounded.

Visa

I DIDN'T HAVE TO call Clive, my contact with the potential Visa work, as his partner, John K, called three days after I got home with a possibility. Then it took ten days before he could set up an interview and I had to restart my job search. But I didn't have to look long as the interview at Visa went well and they were ready for me to start the following week. The job was to manage the computer operation of a temporary contest. The advertising for the contest was "Use your Visa card and your purchase could be free." The initial task was to review all of the computer jobs that had run the contest the previous year. They had to be tested to make sure that they were still operational and produced the desired results. Then computer operations had to be notified and a schedule established for running the jobs. After the contest started, my job would be to monitor the results of the computer jobs and take care of any problems. Other people got to notify the winners.

Unfortunately, it rapidly became apparent that this was not going to be a full-time job for the seven months of the set-up and the contest. I wasn't even sure I could make it a half-time job. The people at Visa were surprised because the person who had managed the contest the previous year had been busy for the whole time. But I had managed to impress them with my abilities and they found other work for me to do to make it a full-time job. The commute to Visa, in San Mateo County, was about a ninety-mile round trip from my house in Marin County. I had decided that I could do anything, even this ridiculous commute, for seven months. I wasn't expecting it to last over eleven years.

I did have to get a new car. The Fiat Spyder I'd bought in 1984 had over 100,000 miles on it and was starting to show its age. I wasn't sure it was up to the daily ninety-mile round trip. Before leaving for Taiwan I'd decided that my next car would be the newly redesigned Ford Mustang. So I got a one-year-old used one for my commute. It was red. I sold the Fiat to a German exchange student who needed something to drive for the summer. He liked it well enough that he called me a few weeks later to get a formal bill of sale so he could take it home to Germany with him.

A couple of months after I started working at Visa I got a call from Kaye who had worked for me at Rand. She was now the Business Manager for BASE II, Visa's system to process credit card transactions. Business Manager was a great job.

Kaye acted as the interface between the business community and the technical analysts maintaining the system. You had to understand both the business *and* technology to do the job well. We kept in touch and as my first Visa contract was winding up, Kaye offered me a second contract working for her. When she left BASE II for another job at Visa, I was offered her old job of Business Manager. It was a perfect job for me. The only problem was the ninety-mile-a-day commute but I decided to continue doing it. The rest of my life was in Marin County and I didn't want to move.

The credit card business was new to me but Kaye had been a good teacher and I was a fast learner. I was back doing what I did best, analysis and design without having to manage anyone. I had learned a valuable lesson in the two years since I'd been fired from Schwab. I was still the same person with the same set of skills and interests. But now, in the right job, I was again a valuable person in the organization. My problem at Schwab had truly been that I was in the wrong job and this made me look at people who were doing a "bad" job in a new way. It wasn't that they were "bad employees," it was probably that they were just in the wrong job.

At that time Visa had two major systems. One system, BASE II, processed credit card transactions. The other system, Debit, processed debit card transactions. There was considerable friction between the people responsible for the two systems. One day Joe M, my boss, came into my office and invited me to a meeting he was going to with the Debit

Card people. It was a fairly long meeting. A recent problem in Debit Card system processing was discussed. Causes and solutions were considered. Joe and I were the only non-Debit Card people there and both of us found the meeting pretty incomprehensible. Finally, at the end of the meeting, everyone turned to Joe.

"It's obvious it is a BASE II problem, what are you going to do to fix it?" asked one of the Debit attendees.

Without batting an eyelash, Joe responded, "Mary will get back to you on that."

I was stunned, but not for long. After the meeting Joe gave me my real assignment.

"That is never going to happen to me again," he said. "Your only job at the moment is to understand the Debit System so we can be proactive about things like this."

I started my analysis of the Debit System with a memo that had been written to describe the problem discussed at the meeting Joe and I had attended. My reaction to the memo was that it was one of the most poorly written, useless memos I had ever read. But there were other ways to learn about a system and I knew lots of them. About six or eight weeks after the terrible meeting, I asked Debbie, my Debit System contact, a question.

"It's in the memo," she replied with irritation.

I sighed to myself but did go and reread the "awful" memo. It made perfect sense and answered my question fully. I had learned to speak "Debit."

While I was working on this problem, a management position became available in Joe's department. He offered me the job. I must have looked horrified as he followed up quickly.

"It's ok," he said, "you won't be fired if you say no."

Obviously my days of having to turn down promotions to management were not over.

The interface problem between BASE II and the Debit System that we had been trying to fix was only the tip of the iceberg. The interface between the two systems was fraught with problems and, as I had discovered, the people managing the two systems spoke "different languages." Over time two things became apparent to me. The first was that soon, there was going to be a project that would have the potential to greatly improve the interface between the two systems. The second was that the project would be managed by the Debit staff. Since I was convinced that, at that moment in time, I knew more about the interface between the two systems than anyone else at Visa, I decided that I was the right person to manage the analysis and design of that project. If Joe had still been managing BASE II, he probably would have been able to arrange for my involvement in the project. But he had been replaced by Patrick, who had no interest in the interface between the two systems. That meant I had to transfer from BASE II to Debit.

People thought I was crazy. I was BASE II's only business manager with a nice office. I would be one of many service managers working on the Debit System and there weren't enough offices for everyone in that group to have one. But I saw an opportunity to make a difference and in March 1993, I gave up my BASE II office and moved into a Debit cubicle.

Unfortunately, it didn't work out as well as I had expected. I may have raised awareness of the problems in the interface, but in general, I was viewed as an outsider who really didn't understand the business. Part of the problem was my background. I was using the skills I had honed during my years at Rand of being able to understand systems as a whole and fill in the details as I went along. This approach worked fine when you were a consultant and you were expected to know what you were doing. But I was no longer a consultant. My credibility with the BASE II people had developed over time. I'd been in the department for a while before I started making suggestions on how to do things. But I'd walked into the Debit System knowing a fair amount about the system and acting like a consultant. It didn't take me too long to figure out what the problem was. I was acting like a consultant but I didn't yet have the credibility to back it up.

I was never able to improve my credibility with the Debit staff. Less than a year after I moved to Debit, several BASE II people suggested I come back and work on a project to redo Visa's settlement system. I was ready to stop tilting at windmills and transferred back. Later Visa set up a group to manage the interface between the two systems. I like to think that my efforts led to the establishment of that group.

Since I wasn't managing people, it was easy to transfer between departments. My decision to stop being a manager had another major benefit. I had more time for a personal life. Since I no longer enjoyed spending time with Tony, I had plenty of time to spend with my new love, horses.

Chief and Lucky

I WAS FORTY-SEVEN when I bought my first horse. He was an Appaloosa gelding in his late teens, basically a bay with a rump appaloosa blanket. He came with the name of Apache, which I didn't like. In a rare moment of doing something together, Tony, who wanted to be part of the naming process, and I renamed him Chief. Initially Tony was interested in my new sport of horseback riding and sometimes came to the stable to watch me ride. He expressed interest in learning how to ride as well. I encouraged him to take lessons. Unfortunately, he wouldn't stop drinking and there was no way a riding instructor was going to allow a drunk on a horse. After a couple of cancelled lessons, he gave up on learning to ride.

I'd started riding about two years before I bought Chief. My riding lessons had been interrupted by my trip to Taiwan but they resumed after my return. By the time I met Chief I had established a riding routine. On Saturdays I would take a lesson. On Sundays, I would take one of the rent string horses out for an hour ride. Sometimes my Sunday mount was Helen, my primary lesson horse; sometimes it was a different horse.

On that fateful day in June 1991, the ranch owner was running the rent string. She suggested I ride this new horse they had just bought at the auction. It wasn't love at first sight, but by the end of the ride, I knew that this was the horse for me.

Carrie, the woman who taught me how to ride, had approved.

"You and Chief are in sync the way you have never been in sync with Helen or any other horse you ever had a lesson on."

I had Chief checked by a veterinarian who said he was a perfect horse for a beginner interested in trail riding. With most horses having a life span of twenty-five to thirty years, a horse in his late teens was middle aged, just like me.

I learned more about horses in the first week that I owned Chief than I had in the prior two years. I had no idea that horses cared about people. Chief let me know he had a personality. He was "a gentleman" who watched out for me and didn't try to push me around. After the first time I gave him a carrot when I arrived at the stable, he was always standing there alertly waiting for me as I walked up to his stall. I also found out how much horses knew how to do on their own. At some point in his life Chief had played in a lot of horseback games. Shortly after I got Chief there was a "playday" at the ranch. Chief and I came in third in pole bending, a timed event of riding a weaving path through six poles arranged in a line. I was smart enough to just stay out of his way. If I'd known anything we might have even come in first and gotten a blue ribbon. That was our best event but I'd never gotten a playday ribbon before and we won a ribbon in all of the events we entered that day.

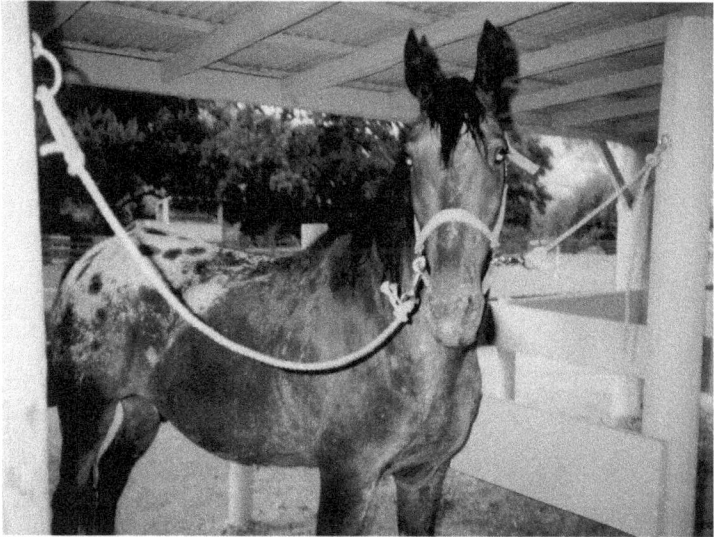

Chief

Chief and I had a wonderful time. My concerns about not having time to own a horse turned out not to be true. I went out to see Chief after work and on the weekends. On most of my visits we went riding. I thought of him as the perfect gentleman. He knew what to do and wanted to take care of me. At fifteen hands two inches, he was hard for me to get on and he never liked being bridled, but these things were minor inconveniences compared to the fun I was having.

Then one Sunday evening, six weeks after our first ride and five weeks after I bought him, I went out to say hi. Chief was glad to see me but not too sure of the dog I'd brought along. It wasn't often I had time for two visits to the stable in one day and I'd been out earlier to ride. The evening trip had been to return something to the stable. The next day about noon the stable owner called to say that Chief had died. I was devastated. Since it was so soon after I'd bought Chief, the stable said they would take care of disposing of the body. But they asked if I wanted a necropsy. I said yes and the cause of death turned out to be an intestinal stone about the size of a softball that had lodged in Chief's intestine and ruptured it. It may have been the reason that a horse as nice as Chief was for sale cheaply at an auction.

So I was suddenly horseless and Tony said I needed to get a new horse right away. After all, that was what we did when we lost a dog. The stable didn't have many horses for me to consider, but there was a Morgan mare named Lucky that I tried out. My reaction after our first ride was that this horse would make me a better rider. I had no idea what I'd gotten myself into.

Carrie had left the stable shortly after I bought Chief to start her own riding facility. So she wasn't readily available to offer an opinion and I didn't seek her out. When she eventually met Lucky she was horrified that the stable owner had sold this horse to me. The first few months after I bought Lucky I became concerned about what I had done. This was way more horse than I knew what to do with. That's a polite way of saying that I wasn't a good enough rider to make riding her safe for me. Horseback riding is a dangerous activity. When many people think of horses they think of the "put one foot in front of the other" rent string horses at a dude ranch. Not all horses are like that. Some horses are firecrackers with short fuses. Lucky was one of those. And even the calmest horse can spook and potentially drop a rider on the ground. Equestrians sometimes compare injuries from horse-related accidents. My worst injuries, a separated shoulder and a dislocated finger, never ranked very high in these discussions.

Fortunately, Carrie was now open for business at her new ranch. All I needed was a trailer to get Lucky up there so I could take lessons. There was a woman at the stable named Valerie who had a trailer. So I made friends with her. Valerie thought that her horse Hilde could use some training. I offered to pay for Valerie's lessons if she would provide the trailer for us to get to those lessons. It was a good deal for both of us. But the best part of the deal was that Valerie's riding partner had recently moved away and she was look-ing for someone else to ride with. She was willing to train a beginner like me to be a trail rider. Again I had no idea what I was getting into. But my ten-year-old athletic new horse was ideally suited to the mad dashes up and down the trails at Pt. Reyes National Seashore that Valerie rode. I just had to learn to be comfortable keeping up with her. I remember an early ride with Valerie on one of the trails near the stable. We had walked down the trail that led away from the stable and came to a narrow, winding trail up to the top of the ridge.

"Ready to go?" Valerie asked and then took off at a dead run up the hill without waiting for a response.

"Should I follow?" I felt Lucky's question in the increased energy in her body.

For a split second I wondered if we could actually run up a steep, narrow trail and then I let Lucky go. Of course we could do that and it opened up a whole new world to me.

Even though horses don't actually speak words, the communication between horse and rider through their bodies can be just as clear as if words were spoken.

Horses could also communicate audibly. If I happened to stop to speak to another horse on my way to Lucky's stall, she would "speak" to me with an angry bray as opposed to her normal welcoming nicker, "I'm your horse; leave that other horse alone."

The lessons and lots of riding with Valerie helped me become more of the rider that Lucky needed. As it turned out Lucky also needed something to help her become the horse I needed. The March after I bought Lucky, I had scheduled two weekend ski trips to our cabin. This meant that Lucky wouldn't be ridden much that month. So I arranged to have Carrie take Lucky for the month and give her some training. When I showed up for my first lesson after Lucky had been there for over a week, Carrie had some remarkable news.

"I was prepared not to like Lucky," she said, "but she is actually a nice horse who has never had any training."

It turned out that Lucky was even greener than I was. No wonder we had problems. As a novice rider I wasn't consistent with my commands. As an untrained horse Lucky frequently had no idea what I was asking her to do. It was easy for us to get frustrated with each other. That one month of training made a huge difference in our relationship. And I started enjoying riding even more.

There were a number of people at the stable that I rode with. In addition to Valerie I acquired another regular riding buddy, Jerry P. Rides with Jerry tended to be slower than rides with Valerie so it gave me a nice change of pace. Valerie and Jerry couldn't ride together as both of their horses had to be in front and whoever wasn't in front had an uncomfortable ride. The reason that they both liked riding with me was that Lucky and I were perfectly happy to stay in the back. I kept a riding log in 1993 and logged 278 hours in the saddle that year. It was a lot of riding for someone who was working full time.

Some of those hours were spent learning a new activity to do with my horse, "team penning." The summer of 1993 the ranch owner decided to rent a herd of calves and set up team penning classes. In this horse activity one member of the team separates one or more calves from the herd and then the team drives the calf or calves to the far end of the arena and into in a pen. It is harder than it sounds. Team penning is a timed event so speed was important, but moving too fast around a herd of calves can stampede a herd and add time to the run. We did penning both in teams of two people with one calf and teams of three people with three calves. Because there was so much going on in the sport, I had no time to think about how scary it was riding a horse and just relaxed and did it. It helped my riding skills a lot. At the end of the training we had a competition. Lucky and I did okay but it wasn't a ribbon-winning ride.

The best part of riding though was that it got me out of the house and away from Tony. It also gave me friends again. With my job being so far away, I couldn't really socialize with people from work. Since Tony was drinking most of the time, I didn't like having people over to the house. Meeting people at the stable and riding with them turned into non-riding social activities as well. I felt that Lucky and I saved each other's lives. I was her sixth owner in five years and horses that don't fit in sometimes end up at the slaughterhouse. She gave me a focus for my non-work life and new friends to share her with. Before I had a horse to distract me, I was starting to join Tony in his heavy drinking.

Negotiating a Divorce

BY MY FORTY-NINTH birthday in 1993 I was married in name only. I had my own separate life and Tony didn't fit into it. I have no memories of his ever attending a Schwab event with me and I know he never went to a Visa event.

The last time I remember anything that even vaguely resembled doing anything together was in the fall of 1989. Tony had bought "weekend season tickets" to the Oakland A's. I went with him to the Saturday home games. Someone else went with him to the Sunday home games. In 1989 the Oakland A's and the San Francisco Giants were in the World Series. Because Tony had season tickets he had tickets to the World Series. We went to the first game of the 1989 Series. The A's won the game. The second game was on the same day as my first horse show. Tony sold the tickets to a friend and went to the horse show to watch me ride. I didn't do well but it was fun and because Tony was there, I have pictures.

The third game of the World Series was a home game for the San Francisco Giants so we didn't have tickets, but that game was also memorable because it didn't happen. We were hanging out in the kitchen with the TV on waiting for the game to start and the Loma Prieta earthquake happened instead. To refute the idea that dogs can sense earthquakes, several seconds into the earthquake, the dogs, Bravo and Chelsea, raised their heads as if to say "something is happening." I grabbed their collars as they stood up and they waited with us until the shaking stopped.

Then in 1993 Tony went to Hawaii for six or seven weeks. One of his friends from the Sixth Army had retired and moved there. This wasn't his first trip without me. Earlier in 1993 he had spent two weeks in Reno on his own. But the Hawaii trip was long enough that I had time to realize how happy I was when he was gone. It took me a while to figure out what this strange new emotion, being happy, was. I hadn't had days of being happy in years. The job was going well. I had friends to do things with. Horses were fun and my home was my home. When Tony returned from Hawaii, at the end of July 1993, they brought him off the plane in a wheelchair. He hadn't stopped drinking on his trip, and he was truly falling apart because of it.

I'm not sure when I decided to get a divorce. I do know that I didn't tell Tony of my intent until early 1994. However,

I went up to Seattle for Christmas in 1993 by myself and celebrated New Year's Eve with some riding buddies. At some point I realized that his life wouldn't change much whether we were married or not. And, that my life would be much better if we weren't married.

I should have gotten a divorce earlier. It would have been financially disastrous at various times, but I would have been young enough to recover. I've often thought I didn't choose divorce because we didn't have children. Many of my current friends are in their second marriage. They left their first marriage for the sake of their children. For me, it was just easier for Tony and me to have separate lives.

I got a recommendation for a divorce lawyer from a co-worker whose wife was a lawyer. In the spring of 1994, after talking to the lawyer, I told Tony that I wanted a divorce. His response was to become sullen and uncommunicative. It seemed like his drinking got worse and I wondered to myself if he was trying to drink himself to death. It was impossible to talk to him about divorce proceedings with him in that shape. In early June 1994, I came home from work to find him sprawled on the floor, unable to get up. I called an ambulance to take him to the emergency room and he ended up spending the next three months in a nursing home recovering his health. This was right before my fiftieth birthday.

Turning fifty was the most exciting milestone birthday of my life. It was even better than turning twenty-one as I was away from all of my friends on that birthday. Part of the excitement over the milestone birthday might have been my pending change in marital status. I was definitely looking forward to being single again. But shortly before my fiftieth birthday, I read something that seemed to put the age milestone in perspective. It said, "Your forties are the old age of youth; your fifties are the youth of old age." It seemed to explain why this birthday felt like a beginning of something new.

I decided to throw myself a fiftieth birthday party. Because of Tony I didn't want to do it at my house so Maggie offered to host it at her house. Mom and Dad came down to help me celebrate. My cousins Don and Ann also came. The rest of the people there were friends from work, past and present, and from my horse community. Many of them didn't know each other. Other than family and Dave F and his wife Deborah, whom Maggie had met Volksmarching, all the other guests were strangers to her. She was being a nice, supportive sister helping me out when I needed it.

It was the first time that my parents and my friends had met.

"Your Dad has a lot of your mannerisms." Janis, one of my horse friends, told me. Then she corrected herself and said, "It is probably more accurate to say that you have a lot of your Dad's mannerisms, but I think of them as being you."

Some of the people at my fiftieth birthday party

I came into work the morning before my birthday to find my office completely filled with fiftieth birthday balloons, banners and other trinkets and lots of things that said "Over the Hill." I also acquired what was to become the BASE II fiftieth birthday tombstone. It said, "RIP Your Youth." One of my coworkers, John C, had acquired it two years earlier and was happy to pass it on to me. I made a point of finding out who the next person to turn fifty was and made sure he got the tombstone on his birthday so I only owned it a few months. When I left Visa almost seven years later, the tradition of receiving the tombstone on your fiftieth birthday was still being honored.

Tony came home from the nursing home on September 10, 1994. His health had recovered. I had him served with divorce papers three days later. The next four and a half months were an emotional roller coaster. Some days I was in deep depression, other days I had hope that things would work out.

I had tried to find someplace for Tony to live other than in our home but was unsuccessful in my search. However, we had a four-bedroom home, so there was room for us to have separate areas. Plus, I worked long hours and went to the stable after work so that it was late before I got home. Initially, Tony complemented my behavior by going to bed early so we didn't see too much of each other. But we had to talk about the details of the divorce and eventually we adjusted schedules so that could happen.

The negotiation of the divorce went better than I could have hoped. Tony's time in the nursing home had dried him out and for a while he wasn't drinking at all. It was an unexpected gift as occasionally I was reminded of the funny, considerate man I'd married. His brother Rick tried to talk Tony into going into rehab, but was unsuccessful.

Still, we were able to work out a distribution of property before he started drinking heavily again. I ended up with the house, all of our debt and a serious reduction of my IRA account. Tony got the cabin, the small amount of cash we'd managed to save and an increase in his IRA account. I added some cash we didn't have to his side of the ledger to make it balance. I figured I could come up with the money somehow. California is a community property state so all of our assets had to be divided evenly.

It was important I keep the house as there was no doubt in my mind that I was keeping the dogs. Tony never questioned that assumption on my part.

The lawyers caused some of my depressed days. My lawyer had recommended a lawyer for Tony and he had hired her.

The problem with my lawyer was that getting the divorce paperwork done wasn't a priority for her. I finally had to have a meeting to explain that, for the moment, Tony was capable of dealing with the details of the divorce. But I had no idea how long that would last. If he started drinking heavily again, the divorce might never happen. Within days I had paperwork for us to sign.

Tony's lawyer kept ignoring the property settlement Tony and I had worked out. She thought he should ask for more. She wrote a letter to my lawyer suggesting that we sell all of our assets and divide the money. That problem went away when Tony fired his lawyer. He never told me why he fired her. I think that Tony, in his own way, was trying to take care of me. He could have made the divorce process a lot more difficult. Still, I was going to end up in terrible financial shape and that was not helped by the fact that I had to pay alimony since I was working and he was not.

I also had a panic attack about the possibility of losing my horse Lucky. I was still taking lessons from Carrie and she managed to say the right thing at the right time.

"Don't worry about it. You could just keep her here."

Having friends for support made the whole thing easier.

Tony decided to move to Hawaii. With friends there, it was a place for him to escape to. I let him take whatever he wanted from the house. It was a small price to pay for the stability I was going to get in my life.

Tony left for Hawaii in late January 1995. I took him to the airport. His sister Rosemary also came to see him off. I left before the plane was boarding so they'd have some time to talk. Rosemary told me later, "I know I've seen my brother alive for the last time."

I sympathized with her but I was glad to see Tony leave and after all of the trauma of the last few months, I didn't want to see him ever again.

Rosemary's prediction was right. Tony's friend Alice called from Hawaii, on July 2, to say that Tony had died the previous night. He had been successful in his quest to drink himself to death. Initially there was a requirement to have an autopsy. I kept explaining to people that I wasn't the one to authorize it. Tony and I weren't related any more. But once the coroner's office was told that he was a heavy drinker, the autopsy requirement went away.

The divorce had left me without any spare money. I was deeply in debt and had to pay a large portion of my salary in alimony. But I had to do something about the house. It had been a place to live but not home for years. One of my first activities as a newly single woman was to get a home equity line of credit. We had eliminated our second mortgage in 1993 by refinancing our first mortgage when interest rates were down. My meeting with a banker to apply for a line of credit was memorable. I was wearing jeans and the banker was another woman. If you had told me when I was twenty-five that at age fifty I would be applying for a mortgage as a divorced woman, wearing jeans and that my banker would be a woman, I would have thought you were crazy. Things had changed a lot in the last twenty-five years.

Tony's death left his estate to be settled. He hadn't changed his will and while the divorce decree removed me as the beneficiary, the backup beneficiaries were my parents and Tony's children. And Dad had been named as the executor. The will had been done about twenty years earlier when things were much different. Dad had no interest in being the executor but my brother John said he would do it. After all, he was named as the executor for my parents' estate and this would be good practice for him. My divorce lawyer recommended a probate lawyer in Hawaii for John to contact.

As it turned out I ended up receiving some of Tony's estate. While he had converted a large part of his IRA to an annuity, I was still the beneficiary of what was left in his IRA. The divorce decree hadn't changed that. Mom and Dad gave me the money they got as beneficiaries of the estate. A friend of mine commented that if I'd just waited a little longer and not gotten a divorce, I would have had much more money. But I knew the cost of being married to an alcoholic and knew that there wouldn't have been much left of me if I'd waited longer.

The surprising thing about Tony's death was how sad I was. I thought I'd used spent of my emotions about Tony during the divorce. But after he died, I remembered the good times and the nice things about him. And his death seemed such a waste.

Exotic Business Travel

IN ADDITION TO this personal trauma in my life, I still had a full-time job working on Visa's new settlement system. One of Visa's most important roles was moving money between banks. When a Visa card was used, the merchant's bank was due money to reimburse it for the money it had credited to the merchants' account. The money came from the bank that had issued the card to the person who spent the money. Settlement was the process of moving money between banks. And since Visa cards were accepted around the world, currency conversion was part of the settlement process. One of the first things I had learned when I first started work in BASE II was the process of buying and selling currencies to meet the multicurrency settlement process. Since Visa bought and sold so much currency on a daily basis, their currency conversion fees were very low. They were so low that even after Visa added a one percent currency conversion fee to multicurrency transactions, most cardholders could get a better exchange rate by using their Visa card rather than paying cash. Every industry has their unique elements and I always found currency conversion to be one of the most fascinating parts of payment systems.

One of our first tasks was to develop a data mapping of all of the information used by the settlement process. There were eight or nine of us on the team but most of the analysis was done by Janet, Martin and me. After the data analysis part of the project was over, I was having lunch with a contractor who had been a member of the team. She added another imaginary trophy to my imaginary fireplace mantle.

"The three of you would have these incomprehensible conversations," she said. "No complete sentences and jumping around from topic to topic. Then there would be a pause, and you, and it was always you, would sum up the conversation in a crystal clear English language statement and the others would nod in agreement."

It was a great description of my ability to help analyze a problem and then to document it.

The thing that I enjoyed most about the process though was that we didn't deal in opinions, we only dealt in facts. If no one knew for sure what the answer was we didn't form a group opinion, we found out what the answer was. I remember a discussion in which two of the triumvirate announced that the answer was "X" and the third member disagreed saying the answer was "Y."

"What do you know that I don't?" was the immediate response from all three of us.

It turns out the lone person saying "Y" was correct. It wasn't me unfortunately.

One of my other tasks on the project was to help sell the new system to Visa's regional offices. We decided to start with the Asia Pacific region. I made my first marketing trip for the new system to the Sydney, Australia office in November 1995. Kaye, who had helped get me hired at Visa as her replacement, was then working in the Sydney office. I arranged to fly to Australia a day early so I would have the weekend in Sydney and she could show me around. However, since things seldom go as planned, the weekend I arrived Kaye had other plans for Saturday and I was on my own. I did some exploring in the area of the Sydney Harbor Bridge and walked across the bridge. I also took a cruise on a replica of the sailing ship *HMS Bounty* of *Mutiny on the Bounty* fame. It was a working sailing ship and many of the passengers helped raise the sails. I, however, had the much more interesting job of having the wheel and steering this large sailing ship down the middle of the Sydney Harbor.

The following day, Kaye took me on a trip to the Pacific Ocean. It was hard to think of the Pacific being to the east. This was November, which is the start of the summer in the southern hemisphere, so the beaches were crowded. We had time to go shopping and I bought presents to take home with me. The presents included boomerangs for other people on the team. My souvenirs were a blue leather Aussie cowboy hat and an opal ring. Evenings and lunchtime provided more time to see the sights of Sydney. I wasn't able to attend a concert at the Sydney Opera House but was able to admire it walking around the grounds and was able to see the lobby. One of the unusual parts of the trip was that I was there during the running of the Melbourne Cup. I was told that the whole country stopped to watch the horse race. I know that our Sydney office did. While most of my memories of the trip are non-business memories, it was a business trip and we worked hard during the day discussing the new settlement system and gathering suggestions for improvements.

My next marketing trip for the new settlement system was in December 1995. Unlike the trip to Sydney, when I went by myself, one of my coworkers joined me on this trip. We visited the Singapore and Tokyo offices. Because of the timing of the trip, we had a free day and chose to spend it in Singapore. I was fascinated by Singapore. The combination of the modern Chinese influence, the earlier British influence and the even earlier Malay influence created a city of interesting contrasts. It was a city with a small land area and thus it had many high rises for housing and business offices. But it also contained a large and wonderful bird sanctuary that, in spite of being in the tropics, even had an area for penguins. Unfortunately we got there too late to see the early morning exhibit of an assortment of raptors displaying their hunting skills. Several years later I made a second trip to Singapore in June. Since Singapore is only two degrees north of the equator, the weather was the same except for a torrential rain storm during one of the trips.

Just like in Sydney, the days in Singapore were spent explaining the new settlement system to the Visa staff there and gathering suggestions for improvements. By now we had a polished presentation to give and it was easy to repeat the presentation at our final stop in Tokyo. One of the surprises of the trip was that it took us almost a full day to get from Singapore to Tokyo. And since we were traveling north, we went from the tropics to winter. Even with all of the traveling I'd done, my grasp of Asian geography was pretty incomplete before this trip.

It had been thirty-three years since I had been in Japan after my graduation from high school. Nothing looked the same and Japan had gone from being a place where you could buy electronics cheaply to being very expensive. The staff in our Tokyo office was young and after I mentioned how long it had been since I'd been to Japan, I realized that many of them hadn't even been born then. Having chosen to spend our free day in Singapore, we had no time for sightseeing in Tokyo. That wasn't an issue as much of what we saw during our lunch breaks seemed similar to a large city anywhere else in the world.

The marketing trips for the new settlement system continued, but I wasn't part of any additional trips. Janet, who I had worked well with during the design phase of the project, had transferred into a new area that was spearheading Visa's involvement in the new world of chip cards and wanted me to join her. She had to convince her boss, Virgil, that I would be a great addition to his staff. She also had to convince me that what they were doing would be fun.

Janet had left the settlement system project because in one of the periodic management shuffles we acquired a new boss. She was a nice young woman but technically inexperienced. When she offered Janet and me her technical advice, we treated her suggestions like any other input we received. We used what was useful and ignored the rest. This caused problems with our new boss as she thought we were being disrespectful. Janet solved the problem by leaving the department. I temporarily solved the problem by taking a management job. I was tired of having my opinion ignored because I wasn't a manager. I quickly realize that I'd made a mistake and when Janet approached me about the job change, I was ready to move. So, in early 1996, I changed jobs again to become a Senior Planner in Visa's Technology Solutions Department. I would be working on a new product called "Visa Cash."

Chip Cards

CHIP CARDS ARE plastic payment cards with a small computer chip embedded in them. In the mid-1990s Visa became involved with chip cards with two products. The first product was to add a chip to a Visa card. The purpose of the new chip was to enhance the security of a Visa card when it was used to make a payment. The second product, which was called Visa Cash, was to actually load money onto a payment card that was not tied to a person. It was referred to as an "electronic purse." The money on the card could then be spent in an anonymous fashion, just like the cash in your pocket. Visa had licensed the electronic purse system developed by Danmont, a Danish company, as the basis for Visa Cash. While I was working on chip cards at Visa, I was traveling a lot again. My first trip was to Denmark, country number twenty, to meet the original developers of "our" system.

I started working in the Visa Cash area in early 1996. The rest of the department was then focused on having our first cards working by the start of the Atlanta Olympics in mid-July. Adding a new person to that development would have slowed things down so I was assigned the job of starting part of the design of the next version of Visa Cash cards. Unlike the cards for the Atlanta Olympics which were disposable after the money loaded on them was spent, the new cards would allow additional money to be added to the cards which would make them reusable and thus more cost effective.

I was tasked with designing the process that would generate the individual keys for each Visa Cash card and place those keys and other data onto the computer chip in the card. The high-level design had been already done by Al, one of the senior people in the department. Al and I were eventually to share a United States Patent for our work in developing this process.

Cryptography and encryption were not subjects I knew much about. But Al, his boss Irv and others in the department had been researching what we needed to do in this area so there was no need for me to become an expert. But I learned a lot about data security as a result of the project. The actual generation of the keys was pretty easy from my point of view. Companies existed that built machines to create subordinate keys from master keys and all my part of the project had to do was use one of these machines.

The part of the payment system business that I found myself in the middle of was an area called "card personalization" or "personalization." This process had been around for a long time and there were companies who specialized in it. The basic process was taking a piece of card stock and printing and/or embossing data like the customer's name and card number on the blank card stock. In addition, a small amount of data was added to the magnetic stripe on the back of the card. It was a pretty straightforward, well-understood process. I was soon to find myself one of a few people who understood the impact that chip cards, with their large volume of data, were going to have on the existing process. It was brought home to me one day how much what we were doing was on the forefront of the need to change the personalization process. I was meeting with a group from one of the personalization vendors. One of the men was talking about implementing one of my suggestions.

"My boss asked why I was doing it that way and I told him it was because Mary said that was how it was done." he said.

It was scary going from knowing nothing to being an expert in a matter of months.

The computer process I defined to add the Visa Cash chip card requirements to the personalization data flow was called "P3." I think the official name of the program was "Personalization Preparation Process" so it's not surprising that it got shortened to P3. I added a requirement to the process that no one else was thinking about. It was obvious to me that we were going to have chip cards that had both a credit/debit application on it and Visa Cash. No one else was thinking about it and while I certainly had no authorization to produce software for the credit/debit people, I made sure the software we were building was flexible enough to combine two data flows for the two products and, if necessary, generate their keys for their application. I was pretty proud of P3 and, other than the initial complaints from the credit/debit people about my invading their turf, it was well received by all parties. As a result of my work, a new term "common personalization" entered the group's vocabulary. Everyone realized we had to standardize what we were doing across all products.

One of the benefits of working on the project was that the Visa cafeteria was one of our test sites. So we could use Visa Cash cards in the cafeteria.

One of my favorite benefits of the card was that a twenty-dollar bill doesn't take up much space until you start to spend it. A twenty-dollar Visa Cash card takes up the same amount of space even after you start to spend it. All of your change stays on the card.

Whenever we had visitors we didn't need to worry about buying them lunch, we just gave them a Visa Cash card, which they could keep as a souvenir. Collecting different styles of Visa Cash cards became a quest. I don't have a complete set of those used at the 1996 Atlanta Olympics but I do have a lot of them.

We started out using a type of encryption called DES for our chip card security. However, after a while it was decided that we would use a stronger type of encryption called "Public Key" instead. The push for Public Key technology came from the European region staff who were much more interested in chip technology than the United States region was. Our first major trial after the Atlanta Olympics was to be the 1997 United Kingdom Public Key Trial. And the United Kingdom banks wanted chip cards that were both Visa cards and Visa Cash cards so P3 had to be modified to use Public Key technology. Because most of the cards being issued for the United Kingdom trial were going to be actual Visa cards, the process of collecting them was harder than collecting the spent Visa Cash only cards. I decided that I would have to be satisfied with un-personalized card stock so I asked one of my contacts at Del La Rue Card Systems, one of the personalization vendors for the project, for a complete set of the cards they were going to personalize. I was expecting a stack of cards. Instead a got a framed presentation of all of the card varieties with a printed message in the center that said, "Presented to Mary Gorden, Visa Cash Public Key, 1997 UK Trial." I was impressed that he had taken the time to give the cards to me in such a formal manner.

I was making a lot of trips to London for the Public Key project. Usually these trips were scheduled so that our weekends were not seriously affected. Normally, we would fly on Sunday night and come home on Friday. But on one trip I ended up staying over the weekend. Another woman from Visa and I decided to use this as an opportunity to "pop over" to Paris for the day. The train under the English Channel had recently started running so we caught the first train out of London, which served breakfast, and came home on the last train out of Paris, which served dinner. This schedule didn't give us a lot of time in Paris but we got to see the Champs

Elysee and the Arc de Triomphe. We didn't actually have lunch in Paris as we did a tour of a wine museum and French bread and wine were served after the tour. We counted that as lunch. I tried again to go up to the top of the Eiffel Tower, but, just like on my first trip to Paris in 1967, my fear of falling kicked in. We ran out of time to visit the Musée d'Orsay, the new location of the Impressionist paintings, but we did get to visit the Cathedral of Notre Dame. We found time to do some souvenir shopping and because the United Kingdom was still stamping passports in those days, I have a stamp in my passport that says "Channel Tunnel."

By now it was clear that the United States region wasn't going to do much with chip cards. The extensive telecommunications network in the US allowed real-time authorization of transactions. The additional security benefits of chip cards didn't seem to be worth the extra cost of adding chips to cards at that time. I applied for an American Express credit card because they were offering a chip card and it seemed like the only way I was going to get one.

But the European region's interest in chip cards remained high as they didn't have the telecommunications network that the US had. And Visa Cash was getting some competition in the electronic purse area. Spanish banks were issuing a cash card as were German banks. MasterCard's European division, Europay, was also getting involved. So a new project was started to develop common electronic purse specifications (CEPS). My boss Phil was on the CEPS business committee. Jerry S, another member of our department, and I were on the technical committee. The first meeting of the technical committee was in March 1998 in Brussels.

The technical committee, in spite of our different nationalities, quickly became a cohesive working group. And everyone on the committee was very good. At first I thought that one of the Spaniards, Jose Antonio, was limited in his skills. He didn't say much. But that view of him ended when we were struggling with the "load additional money on the card" process. The Germans had set forth what seemed to be rather draconian requirements that we had to satisfy. Jose Antonio was the one to grasp the underlying requirement that I had been unable to see and the Germans had been unable to state clearly. Once he had done that, the rest of the documentation of what had to be done was easy. What had caused the initial false impression was that his English wasn't as good as that of the other Europeans. Of course we were working in English because the Americans on the committee, Jerry S and I, only spoke English.

One of the interesting things that I learned on the project was that the different national stereotypes had a basis in reality. You would never confuse a reserved German with an outgoing Spaniard and the two Belgian men were also different, one being from the French part of Belgium and the other from the Flemish part. And it wasn't appearance that I was focusing on. It was ways of thinking and speaking and also mannerisms that were different. For example, our face-to-face meetings were usually several months apart. The Spaniards always greeted me at the start of these meeting like a long-lost friend with a kiss on both cheeks. The Germans were more reserved, usually a handshake, sometimes no contact at all.

I became the keeper of the document that we produced. I viewed my role as that of editor, making sure that everything got into the document and that it was consistent throughout. But in spite of the fact that everyone was doing some of the writing, a lot of the writing work fell to me. I had chosen that role for myself partially because I knew I had the skills to do the job. And partially because it allowed Visa more control over what actually went into the document.

Each organization working on CEPS had its own set of requirements to go into the common specifications. After all, everyone wanted to minimize the changes they would have to make to their system to conform to CEPS. The most friction was between Visa and ZKA, the German organization. They had very strict controls on their system and implementing those controls at all Visa terminals would have been cost prohibitive for us. Fortunately, the Germans on the team understood the difference between a requirement—what the system was required to do—and the current implementation of that requirement. Plus Jerry was an excellent designer. He was able to come up with alternate solutions that Visa could implement and ZKA would accept as meeting their requirements. Jerry was helped in this task by Brigitte, the senior member of the ZKA team. She was also an excellent designer. None of this was easy but the phrase "work with me on this" described their approach in resolving the conflicts.

We worked with tight deadlines for the entire CEPS project, but I made sure I still had time in my life to ride my horse.

Endurance Rides

A BIG PART of my life outside of work was horseback riding. Owning a horse had given me a new way of making friends. During the initial part of my riding career, I'd been a solitary rider. But buying Lucky had changed that as she was way too much horse for me to ride by myself on long rides. Gradually riding became almost all of my non-work life. With a few exceptions, all of my non-work friends were riding buddies. For a long time my weekends were devoted to riding. I would take a lesson on Saturday and frequently go for a "short" ride after the lesson. The short rides were usually an hour or two. Sunday was the day for long rides. We would load the horses into trailers and go someplace, frequently Pt. Reyes National Seashore, and take a "long" ride, usually up to four or five hours.

I had taken up riding because I needed a summer activity to complete my outdoor life since I was skiing in the winter.

But by 1995 horseback riding had become my year-round sport and I was no longer skiing. Initially riding was just physical activity to balance the mental activity of my job, but I quickly learned that horseback riding required its own intense mental activity, which allowed me to completely shut work problems out of my brain. Before horses the only reliable way to do that had been to exhaust myself, usually by taking a long walk. But taking riding lessons required an intense focus. There was a pattern to my learning. I would suddenly realize that Carrie, my instructor, was telling me to do something new. Then I would find myself doing that new thing an instant before she told me to do it. Then she would stop telling me except when I got sloppy and forgot to do the proper thing. And I learned the difference between "passengering" and riding. You could just be a passenger on the back of a horse and not pay much attention to what was going on. Or you could "ride," becoming the brains directing one thousand pounds of powerful animal over a variety of terrain at different speeds under changing conditions. Being a rider was more fun than being a passenger and it was a mental as well as a physical activity.

For a long time my trailering trips required I go riding with a friend who had a trailer. But with Tony's death, my financial situation improved immensely. I was no longer paying him almost $1100 a month in alimony. So I decided to get a truck and trailer of my own. In late August 1995 I became the proud owner of a light blue Chevy ¾-ton truck with an extended cab. It was a two-wheel drive truck because getting a four-wheel drive vehicle seemed unnecessary. In all the years I'd trailered with Valerie and Jerry P, they had both used their four-wheel drive feature once each. Jerry let me borrow his trailer to practice horse hauling with my new truck. There was a lot to learn.

After Christmas 1995 I finally ordered my own trailer. It was a white Morgan Built two-horse slant load trailer with dark blue decorations. Since they had a three-horse version of the trailer on the lot, I had checked out the basic trailer design and decided it was what I wanted. I then ordered a two-horse trailer with the specific features that I wanted, like a padded divider between horses.

Lucky didn't like the new trailer. It probably didn't smell right as no horses had yet pooped in it. Of course I'd had trouble loading Lucky into trailers for the entire time I'd owned her. I had been hoping that with a trailer of our own, which we would consistently use, she would get better. But she didn't. The "trailer wars," as I called the process of getting Lucky into a trailer, were to continue at some level for the rest of her life.

With a trailer of my own, I acquired more flexibility. I could ride from remote trailheads with people and not have to use their trailer. I could take Lucky to clinics.

I could also look for a new stable where I could board Lucky. Initially, the stable where I had bought Chief and Lucky seemed ideal to me. There were lots of people around who knew much more than I did about horses and there were lots of trails you could ride without having a trailer. But the owners couldn't keep decent staff. And there were seventy or eighty horses boarded there so the owners had to have staff to keep the place going. I was getting tired of the lack of cleanliness of Lucky's stall. I found a nice little stable that was only a five-minute drive from my house, fifteen minutes closer than Lucky's current stable. It was small, about twenty horses. It wasn't a full-service boarding stable. You had to buy your own hay and muck your horse's stall. The owner fed in the morning and the boarders took turns feeding in the evening. It seemed nice but they were full.

Having a trailer also allowed me to try endurance riding. This sport, which had started in the mid-1950s, involved a ride over a long distance that had to be completed in a set amount of time. The most common ride distances were one hundred miles that had to be completed in twenty-four hours and fifty miles which had to be completed in twelve hours. My friend Janis had started doing fifty-mile endurance rides and was looking for someone to go with her on them. I was not particularly interested but she talked me into going with her to a ride she was doing in Nevada in early May 1997. She convinced me I would be useful as she needed someone to "crew" for her while she was doing the ride. Mostly the job was to help her get ready, help her at the "vet check" that was at camp in the middle of the ride and take care of her horse after the ride. The vet check was an examination of the horse by a veterinarian to make sure it was in good enough shape to be allowed to continue. It was assumed that the rider was capable of making the decision about whether or not she was in good enough shape to continue.

I had a good time at the ride and started thinking that maybe Lucky and I could do a "limited distance" endurance ride. The limited distance rides were only twenty-five miles and since I'd done trail rides of over fifteen miles, it seemed like something we could do. Janis was delighted and we planned a ride together for late May. Then she ended up needing surgery and that blew our plan, but she encouraged me to go on a ride anyway. Marilyn, who had the unique distinction of being both a work friend and a riding friend, was available to crew for me on the Oakland Hills Ride in mid-June. She thought taking her young horse, Rocky, to an endurance ride with all of its chaos would be good for him, and I knew that having another horse with us overnight would be good for Lucky.

Before the ride, the owner of the stable near me called to say she had an opening. And one of the busiest periods of my life just got busier as moving my horse to a new stable got added to my to-do list. At work, we were in the middle of the final testing of our first Public Key Visa Cash cards. In spite of that I had managed to schedule eight days of vacation between June 20 and July 6 so I could attend a local five-day horse clinic, do an endurance ride, and go to the third family reunion at Ft. Worden. Plus I was signed up to be in bankcard school the entire week July 13. The only saving grace was that by then the department had added staff. There were experienced people whose job was to continue testing the areas I was responsible for while I was gone.

To minimize time-consuming trailer trips, I left my old stable when I took Lucky to the clinic. She was not happy about the stall she was boarded in but coped. Then after the clinic I took her directly to the new stable. Horses may be creatures of habit but Lucky managed to deal with having three homes in the space of a week. I spent every spare daylight hour at her new stable doing what I could to help her settle in. The horse clinic had its high and low spots. The person giving the clinic had learned to not beat up on horses; he hadn't learned not to beat up on people. Since I had a lot to learn in the class, I got beat up on a lot. Those moments were the low spots of the class. But the class encouraged me to move out of my comfort zone and I was pleasantly surprised to discover how much of a team Carrie's teaching had made Lucky and me. The best moment of the class came when we were riding an easy obstacle course without reins. Somehow it turned into a race with the other horse and rider who were doing the course at the same time. In the excitement of the moment, I forgot that I didn't have reins to steer with. I didn't need them. Lucky just went where I was looking. The subtle shifts in my body as my eyes moved were all the direction she needed.

The Oakland Hills Endurance Ride was quite an experience. I wasn't expecting to get a completion. With a 7 a.m. start and six hours to complete the ride, 1 p.m. was the required finish time. It was, however, 1:38 p.m. before

I finished. But because there were three vet checks, one of which required the horses and riders to stay at the vet check for an hour, they added an extra hour to the time allowed. Lucky was pretty awful at eating and drinking during the ride and if it hadn't been for Marilyn and Valerie I wouldn't have been much better. Valerie had come out for the day and this was good as Marilyn was out riding when Lucky and I finished. It was nice to have someone at the finish to take care of Lucky as I was pretty tired. Marilyn had taken Rocky on a nine-mile ride as part of the sweep rider team. Two or more experienced riders rode at the back of every ride to make sure that there were no riders left on the trail.

I'm holding Lucky at a vet check

Except for not eating and drinking enough, Lucky did well on the ride. She moved out nicely when we were by ourselves and didn't complain too much when I separated her from other horses because I thought they were going too fast. I'm grinning from ear to ear in the pictures taken after we finished; Lucky is grazing. I left for home not knowing what position I finished in and was surprised to find that I had finished eleventh out of thirty-one starters. Not bad for a first ride.

Janis and I finally got to do an endurance ride together in September. She did her usual fifty-mile ride. Again I did the twenty-five-mile ride. It was my first long trailering trip, 223 miles and almost five hours as the ride was at Cuneo Creek in the northern California coastal redwoods. The ride was through beautiful terrain.

"You are in charge of keeping us on the trail; I'm checking out the scenery." I said to Lucky during one particularly beautiful stretch of trail.

I managed to come in tenth on this ride and received a baseball cap with my accomplishment lettered on it. All of the top ten finishers got a baseball cap commemorating their finishing position. Janis gave me a hard time about my award, after all she had done fifty miles and all she got was a paper completion certificate.

I left the ride thinking I could do a fifty-mile ride. I wasn't sure that Lucky, with her bad eating and drinking habits, could do it, though. It turned out to be my last endurance ride. With Jerry P moving to Oregon and Valerie's horse dying in 1998, my riding time was seriously reduced. And by the end of 1997, my dogs had become a priority over my horse.

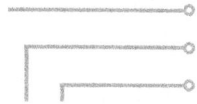

The Ghostbuster Kids

BRAVO, MY THIRD German Shepherd, died in December 1997 and I was immediately faced with the task of getting a new dog. In the past I had gotten a new puppy to fill the empty spot in my heart but this time was different. I needed another dog because my remaining dog, Chelsea, needed a companion. Ever since my divorce, almost three years earlier, Bravo and Chelsea had been each other's main companions. I was gone twelve to thirteen hours a day, there were a significant number of out-of-town trips and a good chunk of every weekend was devoted to horseback riding. In other words, I wasn't around much. The dogs weren't abandoned when I was out of town. Right after Tony moved out, a friend had recommended a very good pet sitter.

This hunt for a new dog was going to be different than the previous ones. Always before we had gotten puppies, as Tony was a stay-at-home parent to the dogs. But now, with my schedule, it had to be an adult dog. The day after Bravo died I had Chelsea out for a walk and she seemed to perk up at the sight of another dog, so I called the breeder I'd gotten Bravo and Chelsea from. They did have a couple of adult dogs for sale so Chelsea and I went out to see them. Chelsea rejected one of them right away but the other one, a three-year-old female, was a possibility. Neither Chelsea nor I were really ready for another dog yet and my first choice was another male so we left by ourselves.

I called the German Shepherd Rescue group and they told me about a two-year-old male at one of the animal shelters. I went to look at him on my way home from work and definitely liked him. But there was a man who was also looking at him who was ready to take him home right away and I wanted to bring Chelsea over to get her opinion. So I let the other person take him. Then the German Shepard Rescue people came up with another dog at a kennel near our house. He was a gorgeous two-year-old and Chelsea liked him. But he was up for adoption because he'd killed his owner's cat. After much soul searching I decided to pass. My next door neighbors had cats.

It was now almost Christmas and I needed to have a new dog soon as I was planning on using my week of vacation after Christmas to introduce the new dog into my life. I decided to call the breeder again and see if the girl dog I'd looked at was still available. She was, but between my visit and my call back, they had bred her. Deciding I could figure out how cope with that, I made arrangements to pick Sparkle up on December 26.

Chelsea's sire had been a champion German Shepherd named Ghostbuster. Sparkle was the daughter of another of Ghostbuster's offspring. So they were actually aunt and niece.

Sparkle proved to have some interesting traits. She slept in the front hall, not the bedroom. It may have felt more like the kennel she had been living in because it was a small space. She wasn't totally housebroken but that didn't last long. At first she was terrified of the wide-open spaces on our walks and when I asked her to go across a small winter creek, you would have thought I'd asked her to commit suicide. But those things passed and she and Chelsea got along fine. The breeders had been two women and Sparkle didn't seem comfortable around men. But my brother Dan and his family came and stayed with us and he took the time to get her over that.

It turned out that Sparkle was pregnant and my first thought was to send her back to the breeder to have her puppies. But my friend Marilyn talked me into having the puppies at home. She pointed out that in addition to my dog sitter I had a housekeeper who was good with dogs. Both of them would be able to come by during the day while I was at work. I could take days off and work at home and use up all the brownie points I'd earned over my years of work at Visa. So I built a whelping box, turned the small bedroom into a dog room and prepared to have puppies. There was considerable irony in the situation I found myself in. I had decided that I needed to get an adult dog this time, not the usual new puppy, but since I got a pregnant adult dog, I ended up with five newborn puppies in my house.

The beginning was a little rough as this was the first litter for both me and my dog. Mostly I caused the problems by helping too much during the births and then again as Sparkle was getting used to these strange beings who wanted to suck on her. As soon as I left Sparkle alone with her puppies, she did fine. After a couple of days when I was sure that Sparkle was taking care of the puppies, she was allowed to leave the puppy room whenever she wanted.

I named all the puppies: Junior, Big Momma, Three, A and B. I never had any trouble telling them apart but then I spent a lot of time with them. When they were two days old I weighed them for the first time. Big Momma was 18 ounces and Junior was 12 ounces with the others in between. By the time the puppies were three weeks old, my scale stopped being big enough to weigh Big Momma who was up to four pounds, four ounces. Junior was up to almost three pounds.

When the puppies were three days old I went back to work for a day. My housekeeper stopped by midday and called me to report that everyone was fine. They were four days old before I was finally organized enough to take the first pictures. However, I did end up taking lots of pictures and when the puppies were twelve days old I started taking individual pictures of them every week. The weekly pictures reinforced the fact that the puppies were growing up quickly. You could see significant differences week to week.

After a week I went back to work full time and for a while my pet sitter came over during the day to check on everyone. The puppies were fine. Sparkle was feeding and cleaning up after them. The only bad thing was that Sparkle stopped being housebroken. Fortunately that phase didn't last too long. And Sparkle chased Chelsea, out of the puppy room. Up until that moment, Chelsea had been the head dog in the house.

After a week and a half, Sparkle got her first walk since the puppies were born. She seemed a little concerned when I closed the puppy room door behind us but she was excited to be outside again.

When the puppies were fourteen days old, I started being worried about A. She had only gained an ounce in the last two days and was now the same weight as Junior, the runt of the litter. Two days later I was really worried as A had lost two ounces and was looking frail. In the same two days, Junior had gained eight ounces. Both the breeder and my vet thought I was overreacting, that she just needed help getting her share of feeding time. However, the next day A was diagnosed with "puppy strangles" as my pet savvy housekeeper found a lump in her neck. Strangles, which is much more common in horses than in dogs, is an abscess in the lymph glands in the animal's neck. My vet operated on my kitchen counter and except for the size of the patient and the amount of yellow puss that came out, it was the same operation that he'd done when my horse, Lucky, had strangles.

After a brief period of not wanting to have much to do with A, Sparkle went back to being her mother again. She watched carefully every time I cleaned out A's incision to make sure I wasn't hurting her puppy. About this time I started referring to her as "Little Miss A."

It was fun to watch the puppies develop. Everything happened so much faster than it does with human babies. At a week and a half Junior and Three started trying to walk. By the time of A's surgery all the dogs were walking.

Before they were three-and-a-half weeks old, Junior, Three and A were all trying to get out of the whelping box. The puppies were starting to play with each other and Big Momma and B had played with a paper airplane I put into the whelping box for Sparkle. Junior got out of the whelping box first. He was followed shortly by A and then by Three. I put another board across the front of the whelping box to keep them in. Big Momma was the first to bark.

Just before they were four weeks old I discovered that the puppies had teeth. When I returned from riding one morning, the puppies were interested in my arms. I'm sure it was the sweat on them. And their sharp puppy teeth scratched me. The next day the puppies got their first solid food, cottage cheese and water. The next day ground beef and rice Pablum got added to their diet. Sparkle stopped cleaning up puppy poop but she still nursed them for a while longer. Another barrier board had to be added to the whelping box as Junior was getting out at will without it. Sparkle allowed Chelsea back into the puppy room.

By the time the puppies were four-and-a-half weeks old, they were incredibly mobile. When I was home, the boards keeping them in the whelping box were removed, and they were going behind the whelping box and trying to get behind the couch before I blocked that off. Sparkle was concerned that they were moving around so much and worked at keeping them corralled. Then Big Momma got out of the whelping box during the night. Fortunately, I had put up the dog gate so she couldn't get out into the hall. After that I put the final barrier board in place on the whelping box.

When the puppies were let loose in the house for the first time they discovered the big dogs' food dishes. They liked the kibble. Then I got worried about Sparkle as she was upchucking. I finally realized that she was just feeding the puppies. About this time I wrote in my journal that I had resolved to spend more time playing with the puppies and less time just cleaning up after them. Eventually, all of the barrier boards were removed from the whelping box as the box had really gotten too small for the puppies to stay in all of the time. Lots of paper got laid on the floor and the dog gate got permanently put up across the room door. Sparkle demonstrated that she could leap the dog gate and get into the room with the puppies. By this time the puppies were roaming around the house in the evening when I was home.

On a Saturday, two days before the puppies were six weeks old, people from work came over to see them. The puppies weren't that interesting as their schedule was to sleep during the day so they could be active when I was home at night. After all, that was my time to play with them and to let them out to explore the house. These weren't the puppies' first visitors as lots of people had been over to see them by then. I wanted the puppies to be well socialized when they went to their new homes.

The day the puppies turned six weeks old the breeder called to talk about shots for the puppies and picking them up. The next day the puppies got their first shots. They also got wormed and there were lots of worms in their poop. My vet reported that that was normal.

On the forty-sixth day after they were born, the breeder picked up all of the puppies except for Junior. I cried. Junior missed his friends but Sparkle let him nurse one last time and he was fine. Sparkle didn't mind that they were gone at all. It had been an incredible six-and-a-half weeks. It was fun watching the puppies change from little black blobs into cute active little dogs. They certainly were a major part of my life while they were there. But once was enough.

I decided to keep Junior because he was my favorite of all of the puppies. If I'd wanted a girl, I might have been tempted to keep "Little Miss A," but I already had two girls and decided I should add a boy dog. Junior wasn't as active as I remembered previous puppies being but since it had been a long time since Chelsea had been a puppy, I thought I was just remembering things incorrectly. Then when Junior was about three months old I noticed a problem with his legs. Dogs normally walk on their toes. The joint that corresponds to wrists and heels in people does not touch the ground in normal dogs. But Junior's wrists and heels were flat to the ground.

It took a couple of months to get a diagnosis. Initially the breeder thought it was just too much protein in his diet so we experimented with dietary changes. And things just got worse. Finally, Jimmy, my vet, made an appointment for Junior at the Veterinary Hospital at the University of California in Davis. His problem was diagnosed as nonfunctioning tendons and ligaments in his legs. They just didn't have the strength to hold his legs in their correct position. I was expecting to have to struggle with whether I could afford the cost of what would be necessary to fix Junior's problem. It never occurred to me that it wouldn't be fixable.

Initially, the doctors at Davis thought the weakness in Junior's tendons and ligaments extended into his bones and that he wouldn't live long. But that didn't turn out to be true and there were ways of dealing with the biggest issue, sores developing on his wrist and heel areas. I discovered a carpet remnant store nearby and basically carpeted the concrete areas of my back yard. This step and bandaging allowed the initial sores to heal and Junior eventually developed calluses in those areas. While the sores were healing and the calluses were developing, I borrowed a wagon from a neighbor and Junior rode to the park for our walks in the wagon. He could handle grass and dirt but not the concrete sidewalks. Periodic bouts of leg sores were to continue for the rest of his life but in general both he and I learned to deal with them. The biggest problem though, was that Junior was aware of his handicap and his inability to move as quickly or as well as other dogs. As a result, in spite of my attempts to socialize him with other dogs, he was always afraid of other dogs. This fear, fortunately, did not extend to his "pack." He always was fine with his mother, Sparkle. And my other dog, Chelsea, and Junior became the best of friends.

Junior and Sparkle

As I was dealing with Junior's leg problems, I also started having to deal with Chelsea's back problems as she was getting old. The carpets I put in the house to help Junior walk also became important to Chelsea's getting around. We tried acupuncture, which actually worked for a while. When it stopped working she went back on drugs. Since I was feeling rich in those days, I took her to a specialist who thought the problem might be solved by surgery. It was like getting a person ready for surgery. The vet did liver tests to make sure she could tolerate the anesthesia that the surgery would require. In addition to x-rays, she also had an MRI of her back. This was done at a local hospital at a time that the MRI machine wasn't being used for a person. The results of the MRI indicated a low probability of success but I decided to go ahead with it anyway. Unfortunately it didn't work. But at least it hadn't made things worse. We put her back on the drugs she had been on before the surgery and they still gave her mobility.

Chelsea was recovered enough that she was social when my friend Valerie came over to help me welcome in the new millennium on December 31, 1999. All of the hype that all computers would stop working on January 1, 2000, turned out to be just hype. The most interesting thing about the start of the year 2000 was the twenty-four hour ABC broadcast, hosted by Peter Jennings, which showed the New Year's Eve celebrations around the world. The first nation to welcome 2000 was the Republic of Kiribati in the middle of the Pacific Ocean. The first celebration I saw on TV was in Australia when I got up the morning of December 31, 1999. Intellectually, I knew that the world took twenty-four hours to celebrate a new year, but it was emotional to actually see it happen in real time. We did not stay up to watch Hawaii welcome in the New Year, three hours after celebrating its arrival in California.

Later in January 2000, Chelsea got very sick and I had to take her to the emergency hospital. It was serious enough that she ended up spending four days in the hospital where she had had surgery after being at the emergency hospital for several days. She didn't improve much while she was there and I thought I was just bringing her home to die. But she rallied. Then when I got home from a short business trip to the east coast, I was met at the door by Valerie, who had temporarily become my roommate, and only two dogs. Chelsea had died the morning before. Valerie, who couldn't bring herself to call me to give me the news, reported that she had gotten up and found Chelsea just barely alive. By the time she had called Jimmy, my vet, Chelsea had died. There was no apparent cause of death, and Jimmy arranged for the SPCA to keep her body frozen in case I wanted to do a necropsy to determine the cause of death. It seemed unnecessary as she was twelve, old for a large dog, and had been sick. But it was nice of Jimmy to give me the option. I was mad at Chelsea for dying when I wasn't around, but at least her death had been quick. I had been expecting her to deteriorate and she had been fine when I left on the business trip.

Saying Goodbye to Dad

THREE DAYS AFTER I came home and found that Chelsea had died, I was off to Bremerton to celebrate Mom's birthday and help her prepare for a more serious impending death. In late August 1997, Dad's persistent pain in his side was diagnosed as lung cancer, it may have been Mesothelioma because of how long he lived after the diagnosis. It was probably caused by all of the years he spent working in shipyards. Dad was determined to beat the cancer; it was his normal reaction to adversity. But almost three years later, it was obvious he was losing the battle. The doctors had installed a pump into his body to dispense pain-controlling medicine. And in 2000 he started using supplemental oxygen. Still, Dad never took a "sick day" and insisted on getting up and getting dressed every day.

I made a lot of trips to Bremerton during those three years. At the very least I was going up for Mom's birthday in

April, Dad's birthday in August, their anniversary in October and at Christmas. In 1999 there was an extra trip as John's stepdaughter, Beth, got married and in 2000 Dad was determined to go to the family reunion. I was one of the drivers for Mom and Dad on both of those occasions. The trips were hard on Dad. The movement of the car made his pain worse and he had so little strength.

The Last Family Picture
In back: John, Dad, Pat, Mom, Me and Maggie. In front: Chris and Dan

The trip I remember the best was one where I was there for a day by myself. There was something minor broken around the house and Dad asked me to fix it. While I was working on it, I was telling him of a problem I was having fixing something at home because I didn't have the right tools. We went down to his workshop and he gave me a box of small screwdrivers. "These should solve your problem."

Then Dad announced he wanted Lobster Newburg for dinner and asked if I would make it. I'm not sure I'd ever made Lobster Newburg before but I knew how to use a cookbook and it turned out pretty well. Dad wasn't big on compliments but by asking for help and not micromanaging my work, it was clear he was giving his approval of the person I had become.

In addition to the trips, there were periodic phone calls. I had gotten in the habit of calling Mom every Sunday. Sometimes Dad would answer the phone or sometimes he would come on the phone after I'd spoken to Mom. He wasn't interested in talking. He just wanted to know what I was doing. This not being the person in charge was new for Dad. At the family gatherings he seemed to enjoy listening to all of us talk rather than telling us what we should think.

By their anniversary in October 2000, he was definitely failing. For the first time, Dad acknowledged that he might not win this battle. He was finally willing to have, what I called in my journal, an "I love you and it's been fun" conversation. We celebrated Mom and Dad's fifty-eighth wedding anniversary on the weekend before the actual event so everyone could make it. Then two days later there was a call from Maggie.

"Can you come back up?" was all she said.

I was in the van pool heading home and made reservations for the next flight out from my cell phone.

It was absolute chaos at the house. Everyone was there. Even some of the cousins showed up, including Kate who flew in from Texas and Liz who flew in from Maryland. There weren't enough beds for everyone so Mom gave everyone their own pillow with a distinct pillowcase on it and we found places to sleep. Someone stayed with Dad around the clock. He was barely able to talk. The hospice people came to make him as comfortable as possible. We tried to take care of Mom but she spent most of her time alone in the garden crying. I lasted four days before I was emotionally shot and had to go home. The next day Mom called. She put Dad on the phone and while he couldn't really talk, he just wanted to listen to what I had to say.

About ten days later Chris called.

"We've lost him," he said.

Mom had been alone with Dad in the house when he died, as Chris had been taking the last of the visitors to the ferry terminal to return to Seattle. But he got back to help Mom through the first terrible moments of being a widow. I called my other siblings and started the phone tree to let all of the cousins know.

I didn't go up until the day before the funeral so I could stay with Mom for a while afterwards. John took charge of executing all of the plans that Mom and Dad had made. Both the U.S. Navy and the Catholic Church are good at ceremonial events so it was an impressive funeral. My sister-in-law Zina secured her place in the family forever when she spoke to the commander of the military detail who had done the seven-gun salute and acquired the spent cartridge shells for Dad's six children to keep as souvenirs. My strongest memory from the family dinner at the house after the funeral is of six-year-old Ben wearing his grandfather's naval officer's cap and saluting. His father Chris was sitting nearby hugging the triangle-shaped folded flag that had covered Dad's casket.

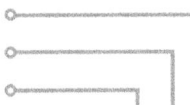

Planning for Retirement

WHEN TONY AND I were divorced in early 1995 I was worried that I would never be able to retire. I was sure that I would be stuck paying off debts for years and would have to continue to pay alimony forever. Tony's death changed that view of my future. But I still wasn't thinking about retiring young. Like most people, I expected to work well into my sixties.

However, by late 1998 I was starting to think seriously about retiring. The main reason was the Visa culture. Visa was in competition with Silicon Valley for talent and, unlike established Silicon Valley companies and dot com startups, they weren't a public company. Stock and stock options couldn't be used as part of the compensation package. Visa chose to compete by offering a great retirement plan. Basically, if you had worked at Visa for ten years and were at least fifty years old, you could retire. The younger you retired the smaller the pension you would receive. There was additional benefit—Visa matched your contributions to your 401K by four-to-one up to 3% of your salary. In other words, if you put $100 into your 401K retirement account, Visa would add $400. Even by the time of the divorce, I had money building up in retirement accounts. Visa's other contribution to early retirement was to keep retired employees on the Visa health plan until they turned sixty-five and were eligible for Medicare.

The other reason I could think about retiring was that the dot com bubble of the late 1990s was a financial boom for many people in the Bay Area. In addition to paying technical people large salaries, you had to give them bonuses as well. Suddenly I was making a lot of money. And with my retirement funds invested in a rising stock market, my retirement accounts were growing. The Schwab stock added to my IRA during my years of working at Schwab skyrocketed up as the dot com investors "discovered" it. I had the sense to sell much of it near its peak and add hundreds of thousands of dollars to my retirement funds.

So by the spring of 2000, everyone knew I was retiring the following year, on my tenth anniversary of becoming a Visa employee. On May 30, 2000, just before my fifty-sixth birthday, I wrote in my journal that retirement was only a little over a year away. I was stressing about not liking the job and stressing about being retired all at the same time. By late July 2000, I was starting to do serious financial planning.

Someone gave me a program that I could use to count down the days to retirement. I'd been using it for a while when Mike, one of my coworkers, asked how many days I had left at Visa. When I told him, he asked, "Why aren't you putting the number up for everyone to see?"

So I wrote the first number, 189 work days to go, on my white board. I do remember thinking "I'm walking away from a lot of money" and the job was still pretty good, although signs of coming changes were obvious.

I wasn't the only one leaving. My coworker on the CEPS project, Jerry S, planned to retire three months after I did. And two other men I worked with retired in early 2001. By spring of 2001, I had spent time with a financial planner and rebalanced my retirement accounts. I learned what my options were for receiving my pension and making withdrawals from my 401K. Since I was less than fifty-nine years old, I knew couldn't touch my IRA accounts without incurring tax penalties so I needed to make my plans without doing that.

The other reason I was planning to retire was that the job was changing. For years when people would ask me why I lived in Marin County and worked in San Mateo County, a daily hundred-mile round-trip commute, I would reply that my personal life was in Marin but Visa paid me well and gave me interesting things to do. However, the interesting things were coming to an end. We had done chip card pilots, we had developed worldwide standards for chip cards and the value of a common personalization process was starting to be understood. The future of the department was becoming implementations and support. I wasn't an implementer or a support person. I was a designer. Plus I was burned out. Lots of long days, lots of travel and lots of impossible deadlines had taken their toll. I was ready to do something different.

The something different to do was to come from my horseback-riding avocation.

Several years after I met my riding friend, Janis, she and her husband Skip bought horse property so they could keep their horses at home. I was surprised to find that I was jealous. That was the first time I'd ever considered buying horse property and keeping my horse at home.

But living in Marin County and having horse property was out of the question. I would have to move. Then I discovered that another riding friend, Denise, had bought property in Georgetown in the California foothills. She was actually planning on retiring to her Georgetown home several months after I was planning to retire. I found out about Denise's plans because, in early August 2000, she was returning a horse she had bought to its previous owner who lived in the town of Cool near Georgetown. Her trailer had problems and she asked me if she could borrow my trailer. I went along to help if there were problems and so I got to see her retirement home.

While we were there we also went to see Brit who had moved to Georgetown from Marin with her husband Stewart about a year earlier. Denise was a good friend of Brit and Stewart and had been instrumental in their move to Georgetown. Because they were horse people, I knew them slightly from their days of living in Marin. I wasn't too thrilled with the area. It was too hot. But Brit said she would keep an eye out for a place for me in the area. It was worth considering. The house prices seemed to be in the range I could afford and my cousins Don and Ann had moved to Auburn, less than twenty miles away, about a year earlier. I would know people in the new area.

Then in early October Brit called to say she had found a place for me to look at. It was a mile and a half from their house, three quarters of a mile from Denise's place. The house was on eight acres so there would be plenty of room for horses.

"Sounds nice, I'll be up in a couple of weeks to see it. I'm too busy to come up right now." I said.

"But it will be sold in a couple of weeks." Brit responded.

Just like in Marin, the housing market in Georgetown was going crazy. I let her talk me into a trip to see the house a few days later. I wonder how much Dad's deteriorating situation was a factor. Looking at a new house would give me something else to think about.

I liked the house. One of its best features was a formal dining room that would easily hold my new dining room furniture. And I loved the land. The area around the house was level and cleared. There was no question where the pasture would be. I was hooked and the following day I made an offer on the house. I had enough cash to cover the cost of two houses until I retired. And the fact that house prices were still rising in both Marin County and El Dorado County, where the new house was located, added some incentive to moving quickly. I wanted to delay closing on the house for as long as possible, but the sellers needed to close before the end of the year because they were buying a new house as well. They did "rent back" the house through early January 2001 so they could spend Christmas in "their house." But on December 15, 2000, I found myself the owner of two homes.

Starting in January 2001, I began working only four days a week and one of those days I was working at home. Because I was easing into retirement, no one expected me to get much work done on my work at home day. This allowed me to set up a schedule of leaving for El Dorado County on Friday and returning to Marin County on Monday. The dogs, Sparkle and Junior, got used to the trips most of which were made in my truck. I got to know Brit and Stewart better and Stewart was helpful in giving me advice and/or recommending contactors for work I needed to get done. My planned schedule initially left me no time to ride, although I did do a couple of rides on Brit's horse Raider. Then, at the end of March, I brought Lucky to Brit and Stewart's place to live. They had so many horses that one more was hardly even noticed. I did pay them for the hay that Lucky ate. It was nice to be able to ride Lucky while I was up on the weekends and to start to enjoy the benefits of my new home.

***

In March 2001 Pat sent me an email saying, "You have to read *Now, Discover Your Strengths* by Marcus Buckingham." And, she continued, "You have to take the test to find out what your strengths are." I followed her instructions. This was the first time I remember using the internet to take a test.

After I took the test I looked carefully at the list of my top five strengths:

Ideation: You are fascinated by ideas and can find connections between seemingly disparate phenomena.

Strategic: You create alternative ways to proceed. Faced with any given scenario, you can quickly spot the relevant patterns and issues.

Maximizer: You focus on strengths as a way to stimulate personal and group excellence.

Futuristic: You are inspired by the future and what could be. You inspire others with your vision of the future.

Intellection: You are characterized by your intellectual activity. You are introspective and appreciate intellectual discussions.

My reaction after reading these descriptions was that I have no people strengths, no doing strengths, but boy can I think. And that seemed like an accurate description of me. I say this to people and they always disagree with me.

"You have lots of people skills," they'll say.

But skills are learned. Strengths, while they can be improved, are things you do so easily it is hard to believe that others can't do them. I definitely recognized the person described as me. Yes, I can get along with people and yes, I can get things done. But what I really like to do is think about things and share my thoughts with others.

But the most remarkable thing about the book was something else. It was, after all, a business book, not a psychology book. So there was a section on managing employees based on their strengths. Under each of the thirty-four strengths in the book was a list of six or seven ways to manage someone strong in strength "X." So I read the sections that applied to my strengths and I was struck by the thought that if anyone had done even one of the thirty to thirty-five things listed under my five strengths, I would not be retiring. It was a stunning thought. Some of the people I'd worked for in my career had been really good managers. And yet even good managers hadn't been able to provide me with that something intangible that would have keep me working.

I hadn't been reading the book as a management book. I'd read lots of management books during my career, most of them while I was struggling to be a better manager. I'd been reading it because Pat had suggested it and once I started, I found I liked its basic premises. It presented me with new ideas that my Ideation strength was immediately drawn to. One of Pat's strengths was also Ideation, being fascinated by ideas. And this book that I was reading for fun had presented me with the most amazing management concept I'd ever come across.

Or maybe it was a concept for living. All of my life I'd been troubled by the common wisdom that says, "No one on their deathbed ever says that they wish they'd spent more time in the office." I had a history of giving up things to keep my career going. What had kept *me* going was this deep need to do intellectually challenging things. When I was allowed to think deeply and seriously about an important issue, I was not only personally happy but I was an asset to the organization I worked for. But that didn't happen often enough and what I contributed was never understood in terms of strengths that could be utilized. I was reminded of my classmate Larry from seventh grade with his wonderful spaceship cockpit drawings. There was clearly a strength there that, if properly utilized, would have made the world a better place. I hope he had the determination to persevere instead of being sidetracked into just making a living.

But I was on to a new project by the time of this discovery. I was retiring to a new life where I could find out what made animals so fascinating.

***

I had plenty of work to do, both on the job and outside of work, in early 2001. I made two more international trips before I retired. The first was to Hong Kong as we were trying to get the Asia Pacific banks interested in Visa Cash. It had been twenty-one years since my first visit to Hong Kong and I saw nothing I remembered. Even the thrilling airplane landing pattern into the Hong Kong airport was gone. The new airport was outside the city and no longer required pilots to slip their planes in over highrise buildings and between the steep hills that rimmed the area.

The second trip was to a CEPS technical committee meeting in Paris. More European banks were getting interested in Visa Cash and other electronic purse programs. A newly added French member of the technical group hosted the final meeting I was to attend. Unlike Hong Kong, Paris had not been destroyed by the construction of buildings made of steel, glass and concrete. Even London had succumbed to this change of building style but Paris had survived. I liked the people I worked with and this would be the last time I would see the international CEPS project team members.

As the meeting was ending, Patrick, one of the Belgian men on the team, said, "Have a good rest of your life."

I didn't know what to say and had to struggle not to get tears in my eyes.

After buying a second house my biggest challenge was getting the Marin house ready to sell. With my job still taking up large amounts of time and having lots of work to do at the new house, there wasn't much time to work on the Marin house.

"I need a wife." I said to my realtor.

As it turned out I was able to hire someone who had made a business for herself doing all the things I really needed done. She located and coordinated all of the needed vendors and was at my house when they were there. She called me with questions that came up and reported status on progress. I still had to do all of the sorting of stuff into piles of things I was keeping, things I was giving to charity and things I was throwing away. But I didn't have to arrange the actual transporting of items to charity and the dump. And I didn't have to be there when the plumber, electrician and other tradesmen came to fix things in the house. And when the painters and carpet installers were doing major upgrades to the house, my coordinator was there organizing things.

While I was still trying to get the house ready to sell, one of the realtors in the area said she had a buyer who was looking for a house to renovate and resell. He didn't need it to look move-in ready. His offer was more than I was originally expecting to get for the house, and the buyer was willing to let me stay in the house until I retired so I accepted the offer.

While all of this was going on, I was getting the new house ready to move into. The master bathroom hadn't been finished and getting that completed was my top priority. There were minor construction chores to do like putting in a dog door, fixing a minor leak in one of the windows and blocking off easy wild animal access to the crawlspace under the house. After the dogs marked the carpet in the new house one time too many, I decided that replacing the carpet with laminate needed to be done before I moved in even if the carpet was fairly new. And I needed a garage.

Plus, since I was setting up a small horse ranch, I needed fencing and a barn. Actually it turned out to be two barns as I really liked the design of Stewart's barn and it had no area in it for hay storage. So a hay barn also had to be built. I also needed to buy a second horse. Lucky had made it clear that she did not like to be left alone. So if I was going to keep Lucky at home, I would need to get another horse to keep her company. By now Lucky was almost twenty and starting to have lameness problems. It was obvious her riding days were limited and it made sense to get a new horse while I could still ride Lucky. After a lot of looking and some tryout rides I bought a young Morgan gelding named Jesse.

Then my buyer for the Marin house backed out. The housing market had softened and I think the buyer saw his opportunity to resell the house for a nice profit decreasing. He stretched the meaning of one of the contingencies to its limit to back out of the deal, and my realtor said it wasn't worth fighting. So all of a sudden, I was about to run out of money. I had scheduled work to be done under the assumption that I had the house sold and the money from that sale would be arriving soon.

I put the barns and the garage on hold. And I talked to my banker about increasing the size of my home equity line of credit. Those steps solved my immediate problem but I still needed to get my house sold. The softening of the market didn't help. But on my last day before retirement, I received two offers and a possible third. I was not going to have to go into retirement owning two houses.

There was one more activity before I retired. It was saying goodbye. Individuals or small groups of people took me out for lunch. There was an afternoon get-together that was billed as, "Say goodbye to Mary." According to someone's count, over sixty people came, including people I hadn't worked with for years. I wasn't expecting anywhere near that many people to show up. The Spaniards sent me a leather portfolio with their logo embossed on it. Europay and the Germans sent cards. As was normal for Visa farewell parties a collection was taken up before the event to pay for a gift. I received a $400 gift certificate at my favorite online tack store. I was overwhelmed. Eight of my closest work friends took me out for lunch at my favorite nice restaurant on my actual retirement day.

On the morning of my last day at work I woke up and had a weird thought.

"This is the last day I'll ever go to work."

Then I decided that wasn't correct, it was only the last day I would go to work at Visa as a Chief Systems Architect.

***

I had done a pretty good job at making dreams come true. I'd had a career I never would have dreamed about when I was young. I'd certainly had an interesting life so far and I was about to begin a life of retirement with my horses in my backyard. It was time to have a new dream. Maybe I could dream about being a writer.

To Those
Who Helped

Acknowledgments

THANKS TO THE late Gail McGonigle, friend and author, for being my first writing coach. She had the ability to say "this is needs a lot of work" without diminishing my enthusiasm for writing.

To Jo Chandler and her "Memories to Memoirs" class who became my first critique group. Gently offering suggestions as chapters started being written.

To Trina Romo who insisted that I could have a readable draft of my book in time for her to choose it as her November 2014 book club selection. She thus provided me with a much needed first deadline. And to the other members of my book club who cheerfully read my slightly cleaned up first draft and shared with me stories of their lives during the same timeframe.

To Jerry Scribner who convinced me that "Girls Don't" was a good title for the first section, but not for the entire book.

To Pam Greer who was always available to edit my latest effort, from the first draft to my beta-read document. And to Margi Dunlap who shared with me as much of her MFA knowledge as I could absorb and who was invaluable in helping me determine the best structure for my memoir.

To Lauren Sapala, writing coach extraordinaire, who managed to convince me I was an excellent writer while making me rewrite some of the most difficult sections of my book. And to Katherine Hitchcock and Mary Myers who joined my team as beta readers.

To Eva Long and her team at Long on Books who made the publishing tasks a positive, if still difficult, experience.

To Marilyn Dyer who provided early encouragement and did a final review of the book under a tight deadline.

And finally to my siblings who, during the entire process of writing and publishing this book, shared with me their memories and their comments (both good and bad).

I couldn't have done it without all of you.

Mary Gorden lives in the Sierra Nevada foothills with her two dogs, Tasha and Darrin, and her horse, Grey. She is active in the local horse community and has developed the bad habit of getting involved in local politics. Recently she rediscovered the joys of programming by building and maintaining her own web site. Check it out at: marylgorden.com.

www.ingramcontent.com/pod-product-compliance
Lightning Source LLC
Chambersburg PA
CBHW051748040426
42446CB00007B/270